The Coming Kingdom

Your future destiny is more dynamic than you ever imagined!

Jim Maher

Other materials available from New Song Ministries:

The Watchman Prayer Manual
Designed to assist and enhance corporate and personal prayer
As Storm Clouds Gather

Copyright © 2005 New Song International Ministries
4103 E. 107th Street
Kansas City, MO 64137

Since IHOP is a registered trademark and has been copyrighted, any use of those letters when referring to the International House of Prayer in Kansas City is strictly for the purpose of word economy.

Cover Design: Cynthia Mitchell of CDS
Book Consultant: Mark Kelker
Book Formatting and Final Editing: Danny Hibberd

Printed by Corporate Document Services
9095 Bond
Overland Park, KS 66214

ISBN 0-9766412-1-6

Special Thanks To ...

My bride Elizabeth who gets the Congressional Medal of Honor for her relentless support and patience ... she prayed while I wrote and that's a lot of prayer

My loving son Reuben and his bride Alison who are mature beyond their years and always seem to have a word of wisdom when I need it most

My precious daughter Rebekah whose happy heart and cheerful spirit impact everyone with whom she comes in contact

My granddaughter Kaitlyn whose innocence and quest for life melts my heart

My awesome sister Bonnie who suddenly found herself filling the role of primary editor

Mike and Diane Bickle whose dedication and tireless service to the Body of Christ have enriched multitudes

Our long time friend Jane Berrey whose cabin allowed us the optimum setting and ambience to write this book

Contents

Introduction

During the early 70's a prophetic book on the last days began circulating through the church. It rocked the Body of Christ in a profoundly positive way. It became the *buzz* of the Kingdom. It created both excitement and genuine interest in God's end time plans. It seemed like everyone I knew was reading the Book of Revelation, many for the first time. They were trying to gain understanding of the events that the Apostle John had forecasted. Although a few went way-off the deep-end and adopted some strange views, most Believers were studying the Word of God with intensity and sincerity. There seemed to be an unusual hunger to go deep into God's Word and search out end time matters. The thing that was driving this desire was that many Christians strongly believed that Jesus could return at any second and wanted them to be prepared.

With the passing of time I watched this passion begin to wane. The reasons for this spirit of apathy gaining a foothold among the people of God were numerous. Sadly, the same people who years before had been seeking truth with an unusual dedication, now seemed disinterested and distracted. Although most continued attending church, it was obvious that their passions had become redirected into other areas of life. Their focus was now centered on careers, recreation or entertainment. Jesus said that if you really want to know where a man's heart is just pay attention to what he talks about the most (Matt.12:34).

I began to ask myself what could have happened to make such a radical difference in these individuals' lives. What had caused them to go from *"red hot"* to *"ice cold"* in a matter of years? Why had they become so bored with church and God so quickly? I was perplexed and struggled to adequately come up with an answer for this disturbing dilemma.

I don't want to exaggerate the matter, but I feel like I am starting to receive some new insight on this puzzling problem. This understanding has come as a result of watching a fresh wind begin to blow through the church. It is totally reminiscent of the early 70's with several exceptions. One of these exceptions is fiery prayer. The Jesus movement of the 70's had passion, evangelism and new worship expressions as its primary thrusts. These were awesome and took a generation by storm.

However, this new move of God that is emerging is a youth movement that is rooted in intimacy and is grounded in fasting and fervent prayer. As this movement is getting established, something surprising is beginning to evolve that is launching this spiritual revolution to an entirely new level. This new momentum is generating a fresh hunger to investigate end times revelation. It's like we've done a huge thirty-year loop.

Although there is a fresh wave of God's Spirit surging across the nations of the earth, watching the tidal shift occur in spiritually-lukewarm America is shocking. One place this is currently happening is in Kansas City at the International House of Prayer. Although there are pockets of passionate young people rising up all over America, Kansas City just happens to be where I am living, serving and watching this spiritual revolution begin to emerge. Although this move of God is still in its infancy, it is quite encouraging to watch it grow. May the many rivers that God is releasing merge into an ocean of revival that will wash the nations with sweet salvation!

This move is authentic, organic, and is gaining spiritual traction rapidly. Imagine entering a room full of hundreds of young people who have gathered for the express purpose to fast, pray and seek God's face with zeal and godly devotion. This gathering I am describing happens seven days a week, twenty-four hours a day, fifty-two weeks a year. While you are woofing down Christmas dinner be aware that there is a group of fiery teenagers that will be fasting, praying and asking God to redeem their generation as a token of His love. This is a joy I cannot adequately describe.

My generation has dropped the baton and are, for the most part, complacent, lethargic, spiritually passive, and backslidden. We have lost our way in God. The sad thing is that most of my generation has become so preoccupied with things that hold no eternal value, it seems like spiritual matters take a r-e-a-l-l-y low priority. These once fiery preachers of righteousness have strayed from the path of wholeheartedness and spiritually are living on life-support systems. They would much rather kick back in their easy-chairs, rent a movie and be entertained, then press into God by fasting, praying and earnestly searching the scriptures.

The heartache is that this new band of zealous Believers is looking for spiritual fathers and mothers in the faith and finding few to help lead them. They are reporting for duty and my generation is AWOL (absent without leave).

You may be asking yourself, "How does all this connect with the subject matter contained in this book?" This growing youth movement is discovering something that my generation discarded. They are unearthing buried treasure that my generation left behind. They are finding great delight in the hundred plus chapters of scripture that contain divine insight concerning the end times. This information is lighting a fire in their souls and transforming their lives in a way that is stunning. It is causing them to see their future destiny in God through an entirely new lens. Eternity is clearer and brighter than they ever imagined.

I believe this was God's desire from the beginning. He inspired sixty-six books to be written that are packed full of prophetic information that is desperately essential for the end time church. He fully intended this material be communicated knowing it would cause a spiritual renewal among His people that would lead to an end-of-the-age revival unsurpassed in power and scope in human history.

The subject of the last days, although greatly diminished in the past by poor scholarship, is now beginning to emerge as a primary teaching tool to ignite passion and instill vision in the hearts of God's people. This is the same method used effectively by Jesus, His prophets and Apostles, to inspire saints throughout the centuries to persevere and triumph while undergoing massive persecution. The fruit associated with gaining living understanding about the last days is time-tested and is yielding a fresh harvest among our young people.

This book is written to take you on a journey through the end times. It starts with what Jesus described as *"the beginning of sorrows"* (Matt.24:8) and ends with the New Jerusalem descending from heaven (Rev.21:1-2). I hope you will be deeply moved by what you discover while on this journey. The goal of this book is for you to encounter Jesus in a new and dynamic way. I believe you will find the Jesus of the gospels and the Jesus of the age to come to be radically more than expected. His coming kingdom is absolutely stunning and I think you will be pleasantly surprised by some of the things you will glean as we explore the Word of God together.

If you are a new Believer, do not be intimidated. God wrote His end time revelation with you in mind. It's part of your inheritance. If you are a seasoned Christian, you have probably heard plenty of objections as to why the last days are too complicated and should be left to theologians to decipher. I have great news for you. Although that deception was a brilliant ploy by our adversary to rob the Body of Christ of much needed end time revelation, God is breaking though and awakening His people with truth. Prepare to get back in the race and run hard again.

CHAPTER 1

Why Study the Last Days?

For many years I avoided discussing or teaching publicly on end time subjects. The odd thing was that I had a private passion, perhaps even an obsession when it came to reading and studying about the last days. I found it both illuminating and exhilarating but dared not let too many people know about my hidden hobby.

I had a reason for my reluctance to openly share. It came from a deep insecurity which stemmed from my inability to justify what seemed plain in scripture, yet appeared to be so out of step with the writings of many popular Bible teachers and biblical scholars. This was both confusing and perplexing.

When end time subjects emerged, it seemed like everybody embraced a different view. Some even classified their conclusions as *"revelation from heaven"*. I've been around long enough to know that when numerous people claim, *"God told me"* and yet end up with a variety of interpretations, somewhere there's a hearing problem. Unable to deal with my growing frustration, I set aside my last day resources and just focused on other teaching tracks.

Eschatologically Emancipated

Not wanting to be overly spiritual but at the same time eager to be truthful, it was like, *"His word was in my heart like a burning fire shut up in my bones; I was weary of holding it back, and I could not"* (Jer.20:9). If there is an expression for being *"eschatologically emancipated,"* I

13

experienced it. Eschatology is a theological term signifying the study of last day events.

I began to have a growing confidence that the light being shed on various end time passages was not deception but truth. Verses that had been obscured for years suddenly made sense and seemed to come into alignment with other sections of scripture. This was as exciting as it was enlightening.

My biggest breakthrough came from the understanding I received from simply being able to trust the Holy Spirit to lead and guide me into all truth. God's Word needs to be the primary source of end time revelation as He has made His intentions both clear and easy to grasp.

> *But the anointing which you have received from Him abides in you, and you do not need that anyone teach you; but as the same anointing teaches you concerning all things, and is true, and is not a lie, and just as it has taught you, you will abide in Him*
> *(1 Jn.2:27)*

Some have drawn false conclusions about this verse and have tried to justify a rebellious spirit by announcing they no longer need to be taught by human teachers, but need only to receive instruction from the Holy Spirit. This is not what the text or the context is implying. That would be a gross contradiction of many verses that affirm anointed Bible teachers as gifts from Jesus Christ Himself (Eph.4:11). Think about it. Would Jesus, raise up, anoint and commission specific men and women to instruct His people, then turn around and tell His people not to listen to them? Sounds a bit odd doesn't it?

Rather, this verse attempts to instill confidence in His people that anyone who will trust the Holy Spirit's leadership can also grasp what God has written. Why would God go through the effort to write a letter to His people and then not give them the necessary understanding to comprehend what He was attempting to communicate? Since most of the earth's population has historically been poor and illiterate, why would the Lord supply a correspondence so complex that only a small percentage of educated people could grasp what He was trying to communicate? Wouldn't that violate His Word and make Him a respecter of persons (Rom.2:11)? That would be the equivalent of the President supporting a law that was written in a cryptic C.I.A. language format and then holding the citizens of America responsible for what had been decreed. We laugh and dismiss that kind of action as silly, yet many Christians have placed Bible prophecy in the *"spiritually elite"* category and thus dismissed themselves from the responsibility to diligently seek God's heart for revelation and understanding (Heb.11:6).

The High Cost of Spiritual Ignorance

Here is my point. One belief that has kept the greater part of the Body of Christ in spiritual ignorance has been the notion that prophetic portions of scripture can only be discerned by the bright and the gifted. Because of this, the enemy has successfully confined the greater portion of the church to the equivalent of eating spiritual leftovers. One might ask, "how so?"

In a general sense the entire Word of God is prophetic in nature (2 Tim. 3:16). However, over two-thirds of scripture is prophetic in a more specific way. How would you like purchasing one of those 10,000-piece master puzzles only to discover that two-thirds of the pieces were missing? Do you think you would be able to construct any image that would even slightly resemble the one pictured on the box cover? Would you feel a little cheated? Of course you would. Why? Because possessing a mere third of the puzzle would only provide you with a distorted view of the true picture. Few have ever considered the implications of what I am expressing here.

Sadly, many Believers have settled for a one-third shadowy portion of biblical understanding when it comes to the Word of God. The scary thing is that most seem remarkably content with their diminished portion.

The message I want us to grasp is that without a strong foundation in the prophetic writings of scripture we will always be greatly handicapped in our comprehension of God's Word.

Another strong reason for studying the last days is because we are actually living in the last days. Not to sound redundant, but I believe that it is safe to say that most Christians haven't reached any strong conclusions about the times in which they are living. How did I reach such a finding? Primarily, I have come to believe this by simple observation. We are clearly betrayed by our lifestyles. Convictions produce actions and actions are the true indicators of belief systems. That said, today's church is acting more like we are preparing for a Caribbean Cruise rather than heading into a gathering firestorm. This is why I stated that actions express true belief; all the rest is simply religious preference. Preferences change with adverse conditions but convictions stand in the heat of conflict.

End Time Objections

The first hurdle we need to address is the list of objections and various misnomers that prevent people from gaining understanding of the last days. Because most people have numerous false assumptions that cause them to struggle with last day issues, I have attempted to compile misconceptions that are most common and have created the greatest spiritual resistance. The list I am presenting is not intended to be an exhaustive one. Rather I have collated thoughts and false assumptions with which I have had to personally grapple and work through. These objections will also be discussed in detail in the broader context of this book.

Objection #1: The Controversy Factor
There are so many different ideas floating around about the end times and most are shrouded in so much controversy, why even go there? It's like wanting to swim in shark infested waters!

Objection #2: The Weird Factor
People who get into the end times get weird! They move to remote locations, buy guns and join clandestine militias. They store strange food products and stand on street corners while holding signs that have odd slogans. It seems like every pope, president and head of state becomes a viable candidate for the Antichrist. Some even claim his true identity can be proven mathematically.

Objection #3: The Relevant Factor
End times subjects are so impractical and theoretical. I need teaching that deals with *REAL* people who live in the *REAL*

world, have *REAL* problems and need *REAL* solutions. End time subjects have absolutely no relevance to my daily life.

Objection #4: The Generational Factor
Every generation of Believers has believed that it was the last one. Why should our generation be any different?

Objection #5: The Jesus Factor
If Jesus didn't have a clue as to when He'd return, how can we?

Objection #6: The Confusion Factor
If the most educated minds in Christendom are confused and argue with each other over the events of the last days, what chance do I have of understanding these mysterious circumstances?

Do You Know What Time it is?

Even a casual glimpse into the end time portions of scripture should cause the most lackadaisical Believer to tremble. Sadly, many Christians have forgotten how to tell time. The Apostle John wanted to make sure the flock he was overseeing knew exactly what time it was. His exhortation was:

> *Little children, it is the last hour; and as you have heard that the Antichrist is coming, even now many antichrists have come, by which we know that it is the last hour (1 Jn.2:18)*

Remember, he wrote this nearly 2,000 years ago. If he spoke under the anointing of the Holy Spirit and prophesied that the early church was living in what he identified as the *"last hour,"* what time do you think it might be right now? That's a very important question. I'm not attempting to be cute or coy here, because how you answer and respond to these two verses just might set the course for your life.

If the Apostle John said it was the *"last hour,"* could we perhaps be living in the final minutes or even seconds? Just a thought. I think a fair answer is that we are living much closer to the end than most of us have dared to imagine.

When speaking to various groups of Christians, I spend a great deal of energy trying to convince them that these really are the last days. One thing is undeniable; we are the closest generation to the Lord's appearing that has ever lived. Based on my study of scripture, I sincerely believe the Lord's return is but a few decades away. I am fifty-seven years old and believe that it is in the realm of possibility that I might live to see that glorious event. If not, I am sure my children and grandchildren will witness His Second Coming in their lifetime.

The reason I am telling you this is because storm clouds of great devastation are starting to gather on a global scale, however, very few people seem to be aware of what's taking place. The entire planet has had several significant wake-up calls recently in the form of terrorist attacks and natural phenomena, but the impact appears to have been nominal at best. It's similar to Elijah's servant who saw a cloud *"The size of a man's hand"* (1 Kings 18:44) and apparently didn't give it serious consideration. Elijah on the other hand, when he heard the report, understood the ominous nature of what was happening and ran like a wild man back to safety. While the prophetic voice is crying out, *"it's time to run,"* I see today's western church still sitting on Mount Carmel, singing songs and going about business as usual, not paying attention to the growing darkness that is beginning to slowly envelop them.

God's Wake-up Call

Church, we have a generation to prepare. However, we are so completely unprepared that it is scary. Jesus accused His generation of this same spiritual blindness. After commending the people for their ability to accurately forecast the weather, He surprised them by saying, *"You know how to discern the face of the sky, but you cannot discern the signs of the times"* (Matt.16:3-4). What was really stunning about that statement was the audience to whom those blistering comments were addressed. He was speaking to the seminary professors of His day. These were the spiritual leaders who should have recognized their Messiah and encouraged their people to attend His seminars. Instead they were jealous and upset because He was able to captivate the hearts of His listeners while they had only been successful in intimidating them to attend their lifeless synagogues.

I am not trying to be negative or attempting to belittle the Jewish leaders or undermine the effectiveness of their worship centers, because frankly, we are not doing much better. Please hear the cry of my heart which is, *"church, something's desperately wrong and we really need to fix it."*

I sincerely believe that one of the simple solutions lies in gaining spiritual insight by studying God's prophetic

Word as it concerns the times in which we are living. Someone might be musing in his heart, *"That seems like an odd and overly simplistic response to the troubling scenario that was just presented. Can't you come up with a more practical solution?"*

Perhaps that is true, but nevertheless, it was the wisdom and the strategy that the early apostles chose to employ in order to motivate their people to run hard after God. The book of 2 Peter is dedicated to serve such a purpose. People's last words generally have great value. They are seldom trivial but express heartfelt emotions and instruction. This is exactly the case with Peter's second letter to the church. He has a foreboding sense of what the Believers will be experiencing soon after his departure. He is very aware that he is operating on borrowed time. He uses language like, *"Shortly I must put off this tent"* (2 Pet.1:14). That is Bible language for, *"I will soon be going to meet the Lord."*

Peter was confident that the early church was well instructed on end-time subjects (2 Pet.1:12). Nevertheless, he was convinced that constant reminders were essential to preserve moral purity in the church. He was so passionate about this that he gave three reminders that are concentrated into four verses of the opening chapter (v.12-15). He made it clear in verse 16 that these warnings were specifically connected to the return of Jesus. He then began to warn the church about dangerous teachers who will attempt to pollute the Body of Christ with deceptive teachings. Then in chapter three he said, *"But the day of the Lord will come as a thief in the night, in which the heavens will pass away with a great noise, and the elements will melt with fervent heat; both the earth and the works that are in it will be burned up. Therefore, since all these things will be dissolved,* **what manner of persons ought you to be in holy conduct and godliness"** (2 Pet.3:10-11).

Peter is making the strongest case he possibly can in order to articulate the massive changes that the heavens and the earth will experience immediately following the Lord's return and Millennial Reign. These cosmic alterations are enormous in both scope and intensity. He follows-up these graphic descriptions with a simple question. Let me paraphrase his statements, *"Since there is going to be an explosion of God's dynamic power released at the end of the age, so substantial that it will totally rearrange the topography of the earth and restructure the heavens above, you really want to be sure your lives are in divine order and thriving with righteous living."*

Peter makes a clear connection between righteous living and the acquisition of revelation about last day events. He reinforces this in verse 14 when he states, *"Therefore, beloved, looking forward to these things, be diligent to be found by Him in peace, without spot and blameless"* (2 Pet.3:14). Can we agree that if we are living in such a way that the Holy Spirit's evaluation of our conduct is *"without spot and blameless,"* one might conclude that we are walking in a high degree of personal holiness and godly integrity? According to Peter, the best way to obtain that level of moral purity is by applying our hearts to absorb large quantities of end time information as recorded in scripture.

You may take issue with this next statement, but I believe that strong medicine is sometimes necessary to provoke us to pay close attention and to embrace certain biblical admonitions. Besides, these are Peter's words not mine.

You therefore, beloved, since you know this beforehand, beware lest you also fall from your own steadfastness, being led away with the error of the wicked
(2 Pet.3:17)

I'll leave it to you and the Holy Spirit to resolve what *"being led away with the error of the wicked"* means, but it is not a promise of blessing. This is the kind of warning that makes an earnest Believer shudder and tremble inside.

My point is that the Apostle Peter is urging the Body of Christ to take serious thought and to engage in strategic study of end time passages. Peter says that to take this admonition lightly is folly. He encourages the church to apply our hearts to wisdom. The closer we are to these events actually transpiring, the more clarity we need to have on these last day subjects.

Conclusion

The study of end time subjects is not optional for those who earnestly believe they are living in the last days. The Holy Spirit will supply the necessary insight to all who are earnestly seeking understanding of the times in which they are living (Jn.16:13; I Jn.2:27). The Apostles made sure the *First Century Church* was immersed and fully grounded in last day topics. It appears that the *Apostolic Team* was convinced that having a people rooted and grounded in end time understanding was the best and most effective way to produce fiery Believers who had little tolerance or desire for compromise and sinful indulgence. Today's western church could learn volumes from the early church in regards to walking in spiritual integrity and personal holiness.

CHAPTER 2

The Coming Firestorm

One of the most terrifying phrases in the entire Bible is found first in Daniel 12:1. It is then reinforced and expanded by Jesus in Matthew 24:21-22. Let's take a look.

> *At that time Michael [the angel God has assigned to protect Israel] shall stand up, the great prince who stands watch over the sons of your people; and there shall be a time of trouble, such as never was since there was a nation, even to that time*
> *(Dan.12:1a)*

> *For then there will be great tribulation, such as has not been since the beginning of the world until this time, no, nor ever shall be. (22) And unless those days were shortened, no flesh would be saved; but for the elect's sake those days will be shortened*
> *(Matt.24:21-22)*

The stunning thing about these verses is first, the intensity and scope of what is being communicated. The second is the universal silence with which the church treats these portions of scripture. I can only come up with a few explanations for our avoidance of these verses. Perhaps our silence is due to ignorance. We have just simply never stumbled across these verses of scripture. It could also be we hold to the conviction that these verses really don't apply to us since we would have been removed prior to these events being released. If that is true then our silence is understandable. Another reason for our silence could be rooted in the fear of man. We would rather be silent than be ostracized for taking a different position. Last day preachers have a tendency to paint in dark colors and it makes some folks uncomfortable. The pressure on Bible teachers to tone down their messages seems to be quite prolific these days.

The only other explanation I can offer is that some have been persuaded by certain prophetic theologians that most end time scriptures are symbolic and must be interpreted as such. This line of thought is problematic because very few, if any of these teachers seem to be in agreement with their peers. This leaves others to conclude that no accurate understanding is available and discourages the average Believer from the pursuit of end time study. This is tragic and has done great harm to the Body of Christ.

The Coming Fire Storm

We have looked at several possibilities of how others have approached these extremely alarming verses recorded in the Book of Daniel and the Book of Matthew. So to what are these verses really referring? They are so incredibly ominous that one would think they would be the current buzz in churches all across America. Why then the silence? I will submit several possible reasons for your consideration.

First I want to be clear on what these verses are saying. Then we will address the reason I feel these verses have been the focus of an inadvertent, spiritual boycott.

The meaning of these verses is so obvious that you have to cover your eyes to misunderstand what the Spirit of God is trying to communicate to His people. A storm of biblical proportions is headed straight for the nations of the earth and there are so few voices in the western church discussing this that I find it incredibly disturbing.

This coming global crisis will make the hardships of World War II look like a case of hiccups. I believe that this worldwide catastrophe will be confronting the nations of the earth in a decade or two. These events will make the graphic depictions of Steven Spielberg's most frightening epic film look tame. It's like the glorious promise of 1 Cor.2:9 in reverse. Instead of, *"Eye has not seen, nor ear heard, nor have entered into the heart of man the* (awesome) *things which God has prepared for those who love Him,"* it will look more like, *"Eye has not seen, nor ear heard, nor have entered into the heart of man the global devastation which God has prepared to be released, at the end of the age, upon a planet of self seeking, pleasure minded, unashamed God-resisters."*

Want to know what the really bizarre twist to this coming crisis is all about? The unique part of God's plan is this: the soon coming global crisis is being motivated by a God who is patiently seeking lost men and women and will go to whatever lengths necessary to arrest their hearts in order to overwhelm and subdue them with His love. The ultimate expression of godly affection will find its full manifestation through a series of divine chastisements that will judge and eradicate sin from the planet once and for all. Are you still tracking with me?

Demonic End Time Strategy Exposed

One of the enemy's primary ways of creating an atmosphere of deception is by perpetrating the lie that God is slack about performing His Word. The adversary will sow into the minds and hearts of many last day Believers a seed of doubt concerning the Second Coming. Peter pleaded with the church to be alert because in the last days we can expect an unholy assault from apostate churchmen that will be aimed at creating unbelief about the Lord's return. Peter's response to this blatant assault on the character of God was to remind Believers that the Father's heart is to reach as many as possible before He releases His Son to return. What some will interpret as slackness, Peter points out, are in reality, an extension of God's mercy. He doesn't want any to enter into a Christ-less eternity.

Do We Really Understand God's End Time Judgments?

Concerning God and the releasing of His end time judgments, I have painfully observed that most Christians, of whom I happen to be the chief offender, are woefully ignorant when it comes to God's activities on earth. I assure you that absolutely nothing goes on that escapes His ever-watchful eye, and that nothing happens without first passing through His all-encompassing will. A recent international crisis made this weakness in our modern day theology crystal clear.

In December of 2004, a violent tsunami swept through the regions surrounding Indonesia. Final estimates put the death toll at somewhere over 300,000. The community of nations responded by organizing the largest humanitarian relief effort ever witnessed in the history of mankind.

One of the interesting side-issues that surfaced during the daily barrage of news coverage was the theological question raised by the media, *"Where was God when the killer tsunami hit?"* Although set forth in context as a question, it was certainly much more than an innocent inquiry. Far from being a sincere question, it was clearly a bold attack on the integrity of God. Attached to this question was the assertion, "If God is truly a loving God where was His compassionate heart during this catastrophic event? After all, 300,000 innocent people suffered a violent death. If God knew about it and if He really is a kind God, why didn't He intervene and prevent this tragedy from occurring in the first place?"

What stunned me more than the obvious attempt to discredit God's redemptive nature were the pathetic responses given by some high profile church leaders, whose names I will refrain from mentioning. Their answers exposed a well-entrenched *"humanistic"* root system rather than revealing strong biblical foundations. It was as though these leaders were watering down God's Word in order to undertake a massive public relations makeover in order to bolster God's image and make Him appear more *"seeker-friendly."*

Please remember that our subject is God and His release of end time judgments. Here are some critical questions that Believers would be wise to begin asking themselves. Although these are extremely basic questions, how we answer these exposes our understanding of God's redemptive role in our lives and how much control He has over His creation. Questions like, "Is God really sovereign? Do things happen on this planet that catch God unaware?

Are negative events simply natural occurrences that happen without God's involvement? Does man's sin have natural as well as spiritual consequences? Can acts of disobedience play a role in producing natural disasters and global calamities?"

Want to know why it's really important for you to sort through these issues now? It is necessary because these kinds of events are only going to increase in both frequency and veracity. For that reason you need to have an accurate biblical filter through which to process them. Some verses for your consideration on this subject are: Deut. 32:23; Lev. 26:25; Jer.8:17; 9:16; 24:10; Ez.5:16-17; 7:3-4; Mal.2:2.

Apostasy or Godly Jealously

One of the clearest signs that we have entered the last days is an unprecedented falling away from the faith (2 Thess.2:3). While tens of thousands of pseudo-Christians yield to their own carnal desires and start exiting congregations in staggering numbers, the good news is that multiplied millions of fiery non-compromising Believers will be taking their places on the wall (Isa.62:6). Tens of millions of love-sick, passionate, fully-committed disciples will be added to the church and engaged in worshipping Jesus. What will be at the root of this mass exodus from the faith as predicted by Jesus and the writers of the New Testament? Obviously, there will be multiple reasons for such a departure. One of the most common will be a growing offense with God because of His end time judgments. Lopsided doctrines of God that represent Him as only being a God of compassion and love will be confronted by the great God who arises to judge the earth in both mercy and truth. God does not need to suspend one of

His attributes in order to enact another. He is true to Himself and will always demonstrate His holy nature in full agreement and expression with His divine justice. Judgment and mercy are not mutually exclusive. In order to be fully God, He must operate in both realms equally. This will surprise many and create the great offense that will ultimately lead to a vast turning-away and facilitate the largest defection from the faith in modern church history (Matt.24:10-12; 2 Thess.2:3).

So, how should these spiritual leaders have responded when asked about God's involvement with the tsunami? Great question and one for which we need to have godly wisdom and understanding for future events of much greater magnitude.

> *The LORD brings the counsel of the nations to nothing; He makes the plans of the peoples of no effect. (11) The counsel of the LORD stands forever, the plans of His heart to all generations*
> *(Ps.33:10-11)*

The vast majority of the 300,000 souls that perished in the killer tsunami represented an entire region comprising many countries and providences in Indonesia. Most were Muslim and were extremely resistant to the gospel. The areas most affected were deeply entrenched in the child slave trade. They sold children to adults to commit sexual acts too graphic and shocking for us to discuss in a public forum. Please do not interpret any of these remarks to imply that God released His judgments on these people because these were the worst violators of His Word and therefore He took extreme measures to deal with their extreme sin. I am not even vaguely hinting at such conclusions. Jesus squarely addressed such foolish thinking in Luke 13:1-5, and I stand by His assessment of such notions.

Way Above My Pay Grade

First of all, I am in no way remotely qualified or equipped to know what God thinks about or how He measures sin or how He makes far-reaching strategic decisions (Gen. 15:16). Secondly, when it comes to sin issues, the United States leads the nations as the primary exporter of global perversion. Although no one from heaven is asking my opinion, it seems obvious that our cup of grace and lack of calamities must be coming to an abrupt end soon. I base that on God's Word. There is a disturbing lack of biblical evidence that we (USA) have any significant end time contribution or international role assignment. I've read the verses used by those who dispute what I just stated, and trust me, the obscure verses they use to support their findings are less than convincing. They generally stretch the rules of biblical interpretation to the breaking point in order to present their illusive conclusions.

Let me attempt to be as candid on this subject as possible. The 9.0 earthquake that caused the Indonesian tsunami was nothing short of an act of mercy by God. Let that stir around inside you for a moment before continuing. "What do you mean by that," you ask? "How can the deaths of over 300,000 people show forth the mercy of God?"

In this same region today, hundreds of Christian volunteer organizations are pouring out record amounts of humanitarian aid. In addition, they are having a spiritual impact by the preaching of God's Word and by the distribution of millions of gospel tracts, videos and multiple personal witnessing opportunities. All this was impossible prior to the walls of water that swept through the nations that surround Sumatra. Tens of thousands of souls have been delivered from darkness and the reports of God's redemptive work continues to be documented. Because of one swift act of God, a formerly demonic stronghold has been penetrated and a window of divine blessing has been opened. Only God knows how long that window will remain open, but currently, one of the most densely populated, yet basically un-reached people groups on earth, has been impacted in a resolute way with the good news of Jesus Christ. Hell has significantly decreased and heaven has significantly increased. That's why I stated that what happened in Indonesia was nothing shy of an act of God's mercy. Eternity will surely bear this out. Jesus said, *"Except a kernel of wheat falls into the ground and die, it remains alone; but if it dies, it produces much grain"* (Jn.12:24). Right now, Indonesia is a grain-producing factory.

Unintentional Spiritual Boycott

As I mentioned earlier, there are two things that stand out in Daniel's prophetic future warning about *"a time of trouble, such as never was since there was a nation"* (Dan.12:2). First is the intensity and implications contained in those words, and secondly, the universal silence with which these words have been treated by the Body of Christ. Jesus did nothing to lessen the impact of that season, but rather He added to the scope of this unfolding end time drama by stating that, *"Unless those days were shortened, no flesh would be saved [this word saved is not used in the sense of salvation and eternal destiny, but saved as in preserved alive]; but for the elect's sake – [the elect are the Believers who are living during this difficult period in history] – those days will be shortened"* (Matt.24:22).

Stop and take a moment to consider what the Holy Spirit is attempting to communicate here. If this verse were located in the Psalms, I am sure it would be followed by the term, "selah". This is a musical term that is intended to cause the reader to pause and meditate on what he just read.

Both Jesus and Daniel testify to the fact that a time is coming on this earth that will be completely unparalleled in human history. It will be so severe that if God did not step in and referee this catastrophe, not one human life would survive. Selah! Let me restate this so it is easier to grasp. If the events that are graphically depicted in the Book of Revelation were to unfold today, and if God allowed things to simply run their course, over six billion people would lose their lives. Do you understand that when Jesus described and exposed Satan's unrelenting aggression towards every human created in God's image by stating, *"The thief does not come except to steal, and to kill, and to destroy"* (John 10:10a), that He was not overstating things. Were the enemy to go unchecked and be given free reign to do as he desired, there would not be one person left alive on the entire planet. This would be a great time to shout, "Thank you Jesus for the cross, for Your blood, for releasing me from darkness and setting this captive free! Hallelujah! Your love is so awesome!"

Unmasking the Silence

Let me share with you why I believe so many teachers in today's church have been silent on this matter. My observations may disturb you, but more than anything, I hope they motivate you to wholehearted obedience. We are all on a massive learning curve so please do not take these statements as though they come from one who has completed the journey. I am simply a pilgrim who is in search of truth. I have a strong desire to see truth expressed with godly integrity, while being clothed in sincere humility, as I live truth out in my life. I have light years of progress and discovery still ahead of me. So please understand you are hearing the voice of a seeker, not an arriver.

I shared earlier in this chapter and gave several possible reasons why there is such silence in the church today when it comes to some of the more difficult passages of scripture that address extreme end time events. My gift of suspicion tells me that a deeper reason for such widespread neglect has to do with the issue of personal responsibility. Sounds like an unusual thing to say, doesn't it? Let me explain.

As we progress through this book, you will quickly discover that the things God has in store for the inhabitants of the earth are both fearful and wonderful. The world's darkest days and the church's most glorious days are still in the future. In fact, we will be looking at some remarkable passages of scripture that you will find extremely helpful and will give you a clear understanding of your future destiny in God. Most Believers have never received any biblical instruction about these matters and remain uninformed at present. Sound like hyperbole? Keep reading and reserve your final assessment for later.

The reason I mention the subject of personal responsibility as it relates to the great silence that exists in today's church is because our view of these events radically impacts how we live our lives. The primary difference between a belief and a preference is the matter of faith. People will surrender their life for a belief. A preference on the other hand is more about the moment and how one feels at a particular season. Preferences change frequently to accommodate various circumstances. I have observed that many Christians hold primarily to end time preferences rather than standing on firm biblical belief systems. We therefore are silent because we are unsure. Our insecurities are further induced by lifestyles that are lived at such a frenzied pace that we find it difficult to stop the conveyor-belt and allow time for meaningful reflection on some of life's more weighty issues. The greatest deception about last day events is that they appear to be far removed from our daily lives. Urgent matters become all-consuming, taking up our time and depleting our energy. The tragedy is that we blink and discover that a decade has rolled by, and we wonder how things got so complicated so quickly. The spiritual issues we will be facing in the very near future demand that we give ourselves *now* to a serious regiment of godly disciplines. We need to intentionally adjust our pampered western lifestyles to line up with the timeless counsel of God's Word.

If the term *"spiritual discipline"* frightens you or causes you to want to leap ahead and find something more interesting to read, I suggest you take serious stock of your spiritual condition. Again, I am not speaking as one who has arrived but merely as one who has begun the journey.

The reason for the great silence can be summed up in a word - change. It seems like everyone loves to talk about growing in the Lord, however, few seem to be embracing change. Change is tough. Change takes time. Change produces change and we really prefer *"comfort-zone"* Christianity. Change challenges. It demands effort. Change is costly and few are willing to foot the bill. If change is something you earnestly desire, then keep reading. We will explore the necessity and power of change in the next chapter. Gaining end time understanding without growing in godly character will only produce well-informed carnal Christians.

Summary

We have been looking at the coming firestorm as prophesied by both Daniel and then reinforced and even strengthened by Jesus. There are many reasons why the church has been unusually silent about this matter. None are based on wisdom and could have severe consequences in the near future if we maintain our present course of avoidance. The church's view of global catastrophes must begin to come into alignment with the straightforward teaching of God's Word. We live in a world groping for answers to difficult and perplexing questions and we need to be ready to dispense godly instruction as the storm intensifies.

> *But sanctify the Lord God in your hearts,*
> *and always be ready to give a defense to*
> *everyone who asks you a reason for the hope*
> *that is in you, with meekness and fear*
> *(1 Pet. 3:15)*

CHAPTER 3

The Countdown

One of the great curiosities of the human race is the mystery surrounding events that will take place in the future. Most look to the future with a combination of fascination and apprehension. On the one hand, we have great hopes for our children and grandchildren, that their world will be more stable and afford many new opportunities. On the other hand, we see a growing number of disturbing global events that make it increasingly difficult to maintain an optimistic outlook.

To appease this concern there seems to be an increased interest in the occult, exploring New Age teachings and an aggressive consumption of all manner of self-help books covering a variety of subjects. The Bible describes our current generation this way, *"Always learning and never able to come to the knowledge of the truth"* (2 Tim 3:7). The unfortunate part of this whole scenario is that: (1) God's Word clearly addresses these anxieties (2) has been readily available for centuries and yet (3) continues to be one of the most neglected resources even though it clearly and accurately identifies last issues.

David Pawson in his excellent book, <u>When Jesus Returns</u>, (pg.2), makes some interesting observations about the accuracy of scripture. He maintains that the Bible uses the phrase "Thus says the Lord" 3803 times. Over a quarter of the Bible contains predictions about the future. There are a total of 737 different prophetic words that contain specific information that can be clearly verified. Of these, 594 (over 80 %) have already been fulfilled. The rest identify events that are to unfold in the end times. The Bible to date has achieved an amazing 100% accuracy when addressing future happenings and is worthy of serious consideration.

Last Day Generation

Out of all the amazing predictions contained in the Bible, none are more fascinating or relevant to the times in which we live than the events that describe the generation to which the Lord returns. The events surrounding this unique happening are clearly the subject of more biblical prophecies than any other single event in scripture. Unfortunately, the Second Coming of Jesus Christ is also one of the most controversial and least understood portions of scripture. Although there are over a hundred chapters of scripture that deal with last day subjects, because of the stigma that end time teachings seem to draw, the Body of Christ remains criminally ignorant of some of the most helpful and useful information found in the entire Word of God.

Although there is much debate as to when the countdown to the last days begins, the Apostle John in 1 John 2:18 introduces a bizarre statement that, in my opinion, makes any discussion of the matter a moot point. John, under the anointing of the Holy Spirit, declared 2,000 years ago that he was living in the *"last hour."* This begs the question, "If John was living in the last hour, what time is it now?" Ever noticed that God's way of telling time and our way of telling time are a bit out of sync? To Him "soon" is a very relative term. "How so?" you might ask. Consider the words of the Apostle Peter, *"But, beloved, do not forget this one thing, that with the Lord one day is as a thousand years, and a thousand years as one day"* (2 Peter

3:8). My point is that in the eternal realm, time literally flies. From heaven's perspective, the earth isn't even a week old yet. Selah.

So, if 2,000 years ago was considered the last hour (in prophetic terms), it seems reasonable to assume that we are living in the last minutes or even final seconds. I am not attempting to get overly spiritual; I just want us to wrestle with the urgency of the hour. My observation is that today's Christian church is either way too preoccupied to notice, convinced it really doesn't matter or is suffering from a strong dose of biblical ignorance (Rom.11:25). Whatever the case, the countdown to Armageddon has begun and it's not even on our radar screen.

It's not a matter of whether or not you are *"into the end times"*. Rather it's a matter of discerning the times in which we are living and preparing properly for the coming global crisis. God's prophetic time clock is ticking and we need to ask Him for wisdom and discernment so we can gain a true perspective of the hour in which we are living (1 Chron.12:32).

In order to simplify and clarify things, I will attempt to put the various end time events into several categories: Birth pangs (Rom.8:22), the beginning of the Tribulation (Matt. 24:4-8), the Great Tribulation (Matt.24:15-22), the Second Coming (Matt. 24:27-30), the Millennial Kingdom (Rev.20) and the New Heaven and New Earth (Rev. 21). These will be discussed in great detail later.

Last Day Focus

There is a very common problem associated with studying last day accounts. Through our studies we can gather much information, gain many new ideas and still

41

somehow completely miss the point. When we begin to look at last day scenarios, it is critical to reprogram our thinking from events, chronology, charts and graphs, etc. to the righteous rulership of Jesus Christ. Certainly these can be useful, but they are not essential. Most importantly, the end times are primarily about the Lord of Glory coming to receive a kingdom that has been promised to Him by His Father (Lk.22:29). They are about the demise of all that oppose that kingdom from being established (Heb.10:13). They are about the purification of His people (Rev.19:7). They are about the in-gathering of the great end time harvest (Matt. 24:14; Acts 2:17-21). In short, they are about the fame of Jesus being proclaimed and displayed on a global platform. Any other *primary focus* will only serve to stimulate our intellectual curiosity and will have minimum impact on how we carry our hearts before God (Ps. 55:19b).

Israel: The Centerpiece of God's End Time Plan

One of the great benchmarks in scripture that served as a clear end time signpost was the establishment of the State of Israel in 1948. The fact that a people scattered throughout the nations of the earth for over 2,000 years could suddenly regather and gain national status is nothing less than a miracle of biblical proportions. There is no precedent in all of human history for such an odd reversal of events. Only God could cause such a strange occurrence. Not only did God create the environment for this to take place but He accurately forecasted this happening in stunning detail some 2,700 years ago.

> *It shall come to pass in that day that the Lord*
> *shall set His hand again the second time to*

recover the remnant of His people who are
left, He ... will assemble the outcasts of
Israel, and gather together the dispersed of
Judah from the four corners of the earth
(Isa.11:11-12)

Although, as we will discover later, there will yet be
a future application of this verse as it relates to Jacob's
trouble (Jer.30:7) the *Great Master Economist* of all ages
brilliantly uses His Word to communicate truth on multiple
levels. This is simply one of many examples sprinkled
throughout scripture.

Someone may ask, "Why is Israel's national status
such a big deal?" The existence of Israel as a nation is not
simply a "big deal"; it's a critical component to God's
overall end time strategy. The entire focus of the last day
events is about Israel's struggle to exist and the nations of
the earth attempting to wipe her from the face of the earth
(Zech.14:2). If you don't have that clearly rooted in your
thinking, you will be lacking an essential part, the
centerpiece if you will, of God's last day strategy. At the
end of the age, the nations think they are assembling
together in order to annihilate the Jewish people once and
for all. However, the prophet Joel gives us a behind-the-
scenes look and makes it clear that it is actually God who is
initiating this great end time drama. He clearly identifies
God's three primary issues with these nations. First, they
have scattered the Jewish people throughout the world.
Secondly, they mistreated them wherever they fled for
refuge. Thirdly, they conspired together to divide up the
sovereign land of Israel (Gen.17:8) and to distribute it
among themselves. Joel makes it clear that because the
nations of the earth have devalued and mistreated God's

covenant people, Israel, they will be the recipients of His swift retribution (Joel 3:2-3). They think their issue is with the Jewish people, but in truth their real issue is with God.

"But I thought the church has replaced Israel because they sinned and broke covenant with God. I thought that the church will be the primary vehicle through which God moves in the last days."

First of all, the covenants God made with Israel were everlasting. If you do a word study you will find that both the Greek and the Hebrew words for *"everlasting"* mean a really, really long time. Sorry, but that was hard to resist. If you have any lingering doubts as to the strength of God's commitment to keep His promise to national Israel I would suggest a quick reading of Jeremiah 31:35-37. If He can't be trusted to perform His Word to the Jewish people during biblical times, are you really sure you want to trust Him to keep His Word to you today? I cover this subject extensively in my book, *As Storm Clouds Gather,* so I'll spare you the rerun.

"Fullness of the Gentiles"

To answer the second part of the question we proposed, yes, the Gentile church will be the primary way God moves by His Spirit in the last days. However, a great deal of this enlightened church's energy will be spent loving, interceding and serving the Jewish people. The Bible term for this is the *"fullness of the Gentiles"* (Rom. 11:25). Many sincere Bible teachers have struggled to understand and explain the term *"the fullness of the Gentiles"*. Some say this was fulfilled in 1948 when Israel became a nation (Isa.66:8). Others surmise this occurred in 1967 when Israel gained control of her capitol city,

Jerusalem. The problem with both of these speculations is that they overlook primary and fundamental requirements before this *"fullness"* takes place.

"What requirements?" In order for the *"Fullness of the Gentiles"* to be fulfilled: first, the full number of Gentiles turning to Jesus must be completed and secondly, the entire Jewish population must turn and embrace their Messiah (Zech.12:10, Rom.11:26). It is essential that they be fully restored to their place of primary spiritual leadership under the reign of their Messiah. Neither of these has remotely taken place.

God's primary redemptive vessels from Abraham to the cross were clearly the Jewish people (approximately 2,000 years). Since the cross, His primary redemptive vessel has been the Gentile church (approximately 2,000 years). At the end of the age there will be a radical convergence of the two. Both groups will be merged into one and will be fully devoted to Jesus the Messiah as well as having a supernatural bond and genuine affection for one another. The Book of Ephesians prophetically identifies this emerging reality as *"One new man"* (Eph.2:15). The Holy Spirit is giving us an important heads-up here. The two distinct groups, Jew and Gentile, are identified as being merged into *"one"* because the unification between the two will be both strong and complete. The downside of this union is that it will take place under extremely difficult circumstances (Dan.12:1). We will look at this in detail later.

This term, *"Fullness of the Gentiles,"* carries with it an understanding that contains both numeric and qualitative properties. Numeric, because only the Lord has full knowledge of the complete number of Gentiles who will respond, in the grace of God, to His redemption invitation.

Qualitative, because there is coming a purity that is unequalled in the church's brief history that will enable God to pour out His Spirit in an unusual way, thus restoring the demonstration (or power evangelism) aspect to our gospel witnessing efforts (Joel2:28-32). There is nothing like God showing up and confirming His Word with signs, wonders and miracles to cause people's faith to soar (Mk.16:20).

One of the great tragedies of modern Christendom is that we no longer can say with confidence, *"Silver and gold I do not have, but what I do have I give you: In the name of Jesus Christ of Nazareth, rise up and walk"* (Acts 3:6). Even more disturbing is that our weakened state seems to trouble very few of today's Believers. Most have adapted and become very comfortable with our spiritual impotency.

However, when God begins to release His *"fullness"* to His church, radical change will be the fruit of this "fullness". It will impact every facet of our lives. Fullness of revelation will massively alter how we understand God's divine plans and purposes. Fullness of relationship will totally revolutionize the way we relate to Him and to one another. Fullness of power will cause us to reevaluate and restructure our current ministry paradigm. Fullness of lifestyle will challenge the church to take serious stock of how we spend our time, talent and treasure, and will produce a fiery people that have assimilated Sermon on the Mount values in both belief and practice (Matt.5-7). In short, the church has some glorious adjustments coming in the near future. However, these changes must be wholeheartedly sought after. God will not release an ounce of His glory unless there are people whose "heart cry" is for more of His presence.

Spiritual Contractions

So, if the countdown has started, what time is it? I served as senior leader in a congregation in Florida which was close enough to Cape Canaveral that you could easily see the rockets and shuttles as they blasted their way into outer space. Countdowns were a familiar occurrence. As launch time drew near, you would see cars pulling over to the side of the road and people gathering in groups hoping to get a glimpse of the shot. All eyes were focused on the Cape. People would have their radios tuned to their favorite local station because there would be a live broadcast of the countdown. With eyes fixed steadfastly on the sky and ears listening intently to the live countdown, everyone would wait for lift-off.

There are many in the Body of Christ that are doing the same. They are setting their affections above (Col.3:1-3) and as good Bereans (Acts 17:11) they are diligently searching the scriptures for insight as to where we are in the countdown. The scriptures are still the most efficient spiritual GPS (Global Positioning Satellite) available today.

I certainly am not an authority and have no corner on prophetic timing, but what I am hearing internally, seeing externally and receiving from other sincere seekers in the Body, give me a growing sense that we are in the season that the Apostle Paul called the *"birth pangs"* (Rom.8:22) and Jesus addressed as the *"Beginning of sorrows"* (Matt.24:8).

Being a father of two, I know from experience that birth pangs increase in both intensity and frequency until the child is fully delivered. Birth pangs are a sign to everyone that the birthing process has begun in earnest. Although I believe we are still at the earliest stages of the birth pang process, I sincerely believe we are experiencing real contractions, not false labor. God has released a series of dynamic wake-up calls and the church, as well as the rest of the world, has been jarred momentarily from its slumber. They hit the snooze alarm, rolled over and now appears fast asleep. I anticipate at least one more *"contraction"* before we enter into the labor cycle. The first event claimed less than 3,000 lives. The second event took over 300,000 lives. I tremble to think what the next event might be.

Peter's Prophetic Warning

I have a mounting concern about the cavalier attitude that I see gaining momentum in many Christian circles as it relates to the end times and Second Coming. Peter expressed great alarm and issued a strong warning to the last day church. The Holy Spirit revealed to him that the last day church would be infiltrated by individuals that he identified as *"scoffers"* (2 Pet.3:3). They would attempt to confuse God's people by generating speculation about the Second Coming. Their accusations would contain phrases like, *"Where is the promise of His coming? For since the fathers fell asleep, all things continue as they were from the beginning of creation"* (2 Peter 3:4).

What was Peter seeing? Why do today's Believers appear to be totally oblivious to this urgent word of caution? Did Peter miss the mark? Is this yet to happen?

I am beginning to see the emergence of a disturbing trend that Peter admonished the *Last Day Church* to detect. Peter was undoubtedly convinced that this mocking spirit would try to permeate the church and steer her off course. Today, the seeds are unmistakably being planted in subtle ways that perhaps within a decade could bloom into full-fledged scoffer material. My point is that resistance to understanding the end times is already taking form.

Why is this so important? Peter believed that this satanic assault would serve to weaken the church and cause her to become short sighted. Without a long view of biblical prophecy, the church is very vulnerable. It would be similar to a Delta Strike Force trying to operate at night without the aid of night vision equipment. Both the mission and the safety of personnel would be in jeopardy. Although this mocking spirit has not reached the level described in Peter's admonition, we must pay attention to today's escalating signals.

Summary

The countdown has started and God's Word continues to be the most reliable source of insight and guidance. It's important that we maintain our spiritual equilibrium and not get distracted by secondary issues (i.e. end time charts, graphs, etc.), but stay the course and keep our gaze resolutely set on Jesus (Heb.12:2). As time progressively moves forward we will become increasingly aware that Israel is still God's end time centerpiece. God has designed a brilliant plan to bring a supernatural convergence as He joins both Jews and Gentiles together into one spiritual reality (Eph.2:15). Scoffers and mockers will infiltrate the church and attempt to entice the church into believing that end time subjects are irrelevant and have no significant contribution to make. Sacred vigilance needs to be a high priority among God's people.

CHAPTER 4

Clarity for the Journey

As we begin our journey into the heart of the last days, I feel it is important to share with you the approach I am taking and explain a few ground rules that will help you to understand. This chapter is foundational and essential in order for you to comprehend the context for the rest of the book. If you have ever taken even a casual look at Bible commentaries and their handling of end time material, I believe you will have a greater appreciation for the method I have chosen to present my findings.

"What does that mean?" I have a great debt of gratitude for those who have diligently studied the Word of God and with sincere devotion have taken the time to record their thoughts so we can glean fresh spiritual insight from their labor. They have my highest esteem as I have received significant revelation from their godly labors.

Unfortunately, there are also a number of Bible scholars who seem determined to do their best to diminish the supernatural aspects of God's Word, to the point that it becomes just another interesting read. They seem determined to turn God's greatest miracles and some of man's most gallant exploits into fables and symbolic gestures that deprive hungry seekers of the truth and create a prevailing environment of confusion and unbelief. Their efforts have done a great disservice to the Body of Christ. Nowhere are the erosive effects of their poor scholarship more evident than in today's churches' reluctance to explore biblical eschatological material.

I am keenly aware of the multiplicity of views that exist when it comes to end time studies. I have been reading commentaries for over thirty-four years. What I will be sharing with you is what I have discovered to be true. I say that with a trembling spirit and hopefully, a heart that is growing in godly humility. Please note that my search and discovery of truth is a work in progress. My understanding and deep appreciation for God's Word is constantly growing and expanding.

Secret Things

Daniel was told to *"seal up"* much of the information he had seen until the end times (Dan.12:4,9). Currently, the deepest and purest revelation of last day events is mostly under lock and key so whatever is shared needs to be taken with that in mind. Many today are fasting and diligently asking the Lord to crack the seals and begin to release a fresh wave of Holy Spirit insight into some of these end time riddles that are surrounded by so much intrigue. We are contending for a spirit of revelation as well as angelic visitations so that we might have *"skill to understand"* (Dan. 9:22) some of these fascinating last day mysteries. This is my heart-cry as I write the following contents of this book. It takes God to reveal God as *"He reveals deep and secret things; He knows what is in the darkness, and light dwells with Him"* (Dan.2:22). Without the spirit of revelation this book would be as boring to write as it would be to read.

Our goal is to prepare a generation to serve the Lord with wisdom, zeal, supernatural understanding and power. I believe that we are living in the generation which will usher in the great King of Glory, Jesus Christ. We may be several decades out, but viewing this from a biblical perspective, we are simply a heartbeat away from His glorious appearing (Titus 2:13).

I will endeavor to keep my comments as simple and as clear as possible. My desire is to equip and motivate you to fall deeper in love with God and His Word. I believe that as we receive divine understanding of the times in which we are living and begin to get a glimpse of the glorious plans God has established for His people (Jer.29:11), that our hearts will be so radically impacted that we will be changed forever for His kingdom purposes.

Face Value Interpretation

My approach to interpreting the scriptures is to take what is said at face value. I believe that the Bible says what it means and means what it says. I will attempt to be clear when scripture is clear and silent when the Author is silent. Having said that, there will be occasions when I will offer some additional thoughts or insights on some of the more controversial and complex sections of scripture. I will do this for the sake of clarity. When I take this liberty, I will strive to make it plain that these conclusions are simply my most informed and sincere opinions. I will do my best to lay a biblical framework for these assertions.

You will discover that the Bible offers its own commentary on matters that many have gone to great length to over-complicate. Remember, God inspired the writers of the Bible to write in such a way that it could be understood by illiterate peasants. The Bible was never meant to be monopolized by the intellectually elite but has always been available to those who are earnestly seeking truth. Many scholars are confounded by the simplicity of God's Word and seem unable to resist the temptation to make it as complex as possible. The simplicity of God's Word and the revelation it contains will fascinate His people throughout eternity. His Word is inexhaustible, unbreakable and completely reliable. We will marvel at its brilliance for ages to come.

As David Pawson, a longtime Bible scholar and teacher states in his book, *"When Jesus Returns"*[1], *"The Bible reveals its secrets to those who read it with reverence and obedience, in humility and with a teachable spirit. It yields more to simple intelligence than to sophisticated intellectualism. It is written for ordinary people in ordinary language (New Testament Greek is taken from the streets, not the classics). It is meant to be taken at face value and taken seriously. When it is, a clear picture of the future emerges."* Selah.

Therefore, we will be taking a literal view of the Word of God and basing our approach on the belief that God is trying to reveal truth rather than obscure it. Take Revelation 4:4-5 as an example.

> *Around the throne were twenty-four thrones, and on the thrones I saw twenty-four elders sitting, clothed in white robes; and they had crowns of gold on their heads. (5) And from the throne proceeded lightnings, thunderings, and voices. Seven lamps of fire were burning before the throne, which are the seven Spirits of God (Rev.4:4-5).*

When the Bible says there were *"twenty-four thrones"* (Rev.4:10), we will believe that John actually saw

[1] Pg 3 – Hodder & Stoughton, published 1995

twenty-four thrones. When the Bible says that there were twenty-four elders sitting on those thrones, we will assume that there were actually twenty-four elders sitting on those twenty-four thrones. When it refers to the golden crowns that were upon their heads, we will assume that the twenty-four elders who were occupying the twenty-four thrones were actually wearing golden crowns while sitting on their thrones. Why am I covering this in detail? Some commentators get so lost in their attempts to unpack all their symbolism that the average reader, instead of gaining understanding, ends up discouraged and more confused than ever.

However, when the Bible makes it clear that the information being presented is obviously symbolic, we will try to make these symbols as clear as possible. Here are a few of many such examples found in the Book of Revelation.

> *"... I heard behind me a loud voice, as of a trumpet"*
> *(Rev.1:10b)*

> *His head and hair were white like wool, as white as snow, and His eyes like a flame of fire; (15) His feet were like fine brass, as if refined in a furnace, and His voice as the sound of many waters*
> *(Rev.1:14-16)*

Was John saying that the voice he heard was actually no voice at all but rather the sound of a trumpet? Of course not. Rather he was painting a word picture that when Jesus spoke to him His voice was as loud and clear as the blast of a trumpet. Trumpets are difficult to ignore. Jesus made sure He got John's full and undivided attention. Also, this verse creates an immense contrast from the Jesus of John's gospel.

Jesus' hair was the color of wool or snow, similar to His Father, the Ancient of Days, which denotes both His wisdom and His place in the God-head. His eyes were like fire, which speaks of His passion and purity. Fire burns up all impurities.

When the Bible is specific and literal, which is generally the case, I will attempt to be specific and literal as well. However, when the Bible is clearly symbolic, I will attempt to explain the meaning by comparing other verses of scripture that use similar language. For the most part, the Bible's own commentary is the best and safest way to interpret God's Word.

An example of the Bible making its own commentary is Revelation 1:20. *"The mystery of the seven stars which you saw in My right hand, and the seven golden lampstands: The seven stars are the angels of the seven churches, and the seven lampstands which you saw are the seven churches."*

Here, Jesus Himself solves the mystery. The *"seven stars"* which John was shown were the angels that God had assigned to minister to the seven churches of Asia Minor. The *"seven lampstands"* were not physical stands that held candles, but represented the seven churches to which Jesus was speaking.

The scripture is full of these examples. Another instance where the Word of God helps bring understanding to the text is found in Daniel 7:8.

I was considering the horns, and there was another horn, a little one, coming up among them, before whom three of the first horns were plucked out by the roots. And there, in this horn, were eyes like the eyes of a man, and a mouth speaking pompous words.

Either this talking horn represents a really distorted episode from *Veggie Tales,* or God has something else in mind. This horn in Daniel's vision was obviously a man. As you read the surrounding verses you will quickly discover that this man will play a prominent role during the last days. We'll leave that discussion for another time.

The Great Theological Divide

It's important for you to understand my position theologically. I will use common terms that will be very familiar to those who have studied biblical eschatology. I will do my best to keep these brief, clear and as easy to grasp as possible. I will endeavor to present my understanding in such a manner that those new to the last day subjects may easily follow.

There are basically four primary schools of thought when it comes to the study of end time events. Although there are variations of each of these when reading various commentaries, these are the four primary views that dominate most of the discussions. The four are A-millennialism, Historic Pre-millennialism, Dispensational Pre-millennialism and Post-millennialism.

A-millennialism (or non-millennialism) does not believe in an actual thousand-year reign of Christ, views most end time prophetic events as symbolic or allegorical and has strong disagreements among proponents as to the meaning of their symbols.

Pre-millennialism believes that Jesus will return prior to the thousand-year reign of Christ and generally believes in a literal interpretation of scripture. There remains strong debate over when the church will be caught up to meet Jesus in the air (i.e. the rapture). Historic, (or Apostolic) Pre-millennialism, views the rapture of the church and the Second Coming of Christ as basically an event that happens simultaneously. This view was held by the early church until shortly after 300AD. It took a literal view when interpreting scriptures. Dispensational Pre-millennialism believes the Second Coming happens in two stages. First comes a secret rapture, then seven years later, Christ returns with His church to rule on the earth for 1,000 years. It also takes a literal view when interpreting scriptures.

Post-millennialism believes that Jesus will return only after a triumphant church has subdued all His enemies and thus hand over to Him a totally Christianized world. This work is currently underway and will take a thousand years to complete. Proponents view the rapture and the Second Coming as one event. This view is also referred to by several other titles, the best known being *"The Kingdom Now"*.

For the sake of clarity, my study of scripture has led me to conclude that Historic (or Apostolic) Pre-millennialism is most consistent with the prophetic scriptures. Because there is so much confusion surrounding these views, let me add some additional information in order to make my position as clear to the reader as possible. By Historic (or Apostolic) Pre-millennialism, I mean that I believe in a purified *Last Day Church* that is walking in apostolic power and authority. The Lord will use this church to bring in the great end time harvest which will be comprised of Jewish and Gentile souls. I believe that the church will be caught up to meet the Lord in the air just prior to the Second Coming of Jesus (1 Thess.4:15-17; Rev.19:7). I also believe in a literal thousand-year reign of Christ, where Satan and his demons are bound. The Saints of God will be ruling and reigning with their triumphant King, not only for the duration of the thousand years, but throughout eternity.

Why All the Detailed Information?

There are several reasons I wanted you to have this information. First, it's important for you to know what most Bible commentators believe. Once you have a basic grasp of these four end time positions you can easily identify the theological perspective that various writers hold. Second, most commentaries spend large amounts of time referencing the different views, and then share their conclusions. I will not be taking that approach as it is extremely detailed and time-consuming. This book could quickly turn into a mini-series (something I don't feel inspired to author). Besides, others have written volumes of commentaries on these subjects and many have done excellent work. I don't want to be redundant. I will act more like a spiritual clearing house so I can save you both time and aggravation. My desire is to take a fresh look at some key end time events, and help us gain both insight and become aware of the urgency of the hour.

I will unapologetically be doing my best to convince you that the prophetic warnings given by both the Old and New Testament writers were primarily directed to the last day generation. I am totally convinced we are connected to that generation and therefore have both a unique calling and awesome responsibility. If this is true then it would be wise for us to pay close attention to the escalating signs occurring in our time. The Bible draws special attention to these and warns us to be spiritually alert. Both Jesus and all the writers of the New Testament testified that these events were intended to be distinctive earmarks of His soon return.

Primary Last Day Themes

We will look at all aspects of the last days in great detail so please try not to speculate too heavily as you will find a lot of unexpected surprises in the course of our study. Please keep in mind that my goal is to convince you that end time study is critical to prepare our hearts for the coming global crisis. Equally exhilarating is when the Holy Spirit breathes life and fresh revelation into our weak hearts. Discovering the real Jesus of the Bible is a mind-boggling experience. Encountering the same Jesus that made the Apostle John fall at His feet like a dead man can be nothing less than a life-changing experience.

It will be important for us to keep in mind that the primary themes of the end times are: (1) the revealing of the beauty and majesty of Christ (2) the purification and maturity of His Bride (the church) 3) The gathering of the great end time harvest (4) the bringing under submission and destroying every enemy that opposes and resists the righteous rule of Jesus (5) the spiritual and full restoration of the Jewish people and (6) the establishment of His kingdom from which Jesus will rule and reign among His people forever.

Remember, when the subject of the last days is mentioned, most of us unconsciously drift into a default mode. When this happens, our thoughts center on charts, graphs, chronological series of events, etc., and by doing so we inevitably miss the mark. The last days are about God's great effort to showcase the glory of His Son and to make His name great in all the earth. They are about the revelation (unveiling) of the God-man, Jesus. The entire earth will be full of His glory and all the people will fill the airways with shouts of Hosanna to the King of Kings as He returns to Jerusalem a second time. This time however, not on the back of a donkey. On a white stallion, leading a stunning procession of His saints, He will establish a kingdom that will ultimately become the everlasting dwelling place of the redeemed and their God! No more pain, sickness or death. Just the unfathomable presence of God and undefiled fellowship with other precious saints who through great perseverance have entered into the promised joy unspeakable - full of glory (1 Pet.1:8).

CHAPTER 5

Last Day Overview

To begin our study of the events of the last days, I want to look at two portions taken from the Book of Daniel. The Book of Daniel is the Old Testament's equivalent of the Book of Revelation. Without the aid and clarity of Daniel's end time visions, much of the understanding of the Book of Revelation would remain hidden. Although written hundreds of years apart, these are companion books and are intended to be studied together. The Book of Daniel is quoted more often in the Book of Revelation than is any other book in scripture. Both share many of the same events and together provide rich understanding for the end time church.

Nebuchadnezzar's Dream

Daniel was one of the young Jewish boys who had been removed from his homeland of Israel and taken to Babylon (currently Iraq). While Ezekiel (the prophet) remained in the concentration camp, Daniel served in the king's court. One night the King of Babylon, Nebuchadnezzar, had a dream that greatly troubled him. He sent for *"The magicians, the astrologers, the sorcerers, and the Chaldeans to tell the king his dreams"* (Dan. 2:2). After he had assembled his group of spiritual advisors he revealed to them that he had experienced a very perplexing dream and wanted their assistance in interpreting it. To make matters even more difficult the king added two unexpected twists to their assignment. First, he informed them that they would be given absolutely no information about the dream. That's right, not a single word or even the slightest hint. Second, if they failed in their task and were unable to reveal the details of the king's dream, they would forfeit their lives. The only good news was the promise of great rewards that awaited the individual who could meet the king's requirement to both tell and interpret the dream. Talking about pressure; I'm sure they all wished they had called in sick that day.

Fortunately for them there was a godly young man named Daniel who had a vibrant relationship with God and had a strong intercessory prayer group that met in his house. They prayed, God spoke, and one of the most profound insights in the Word of God was released. Can you imagine what might have taken place had there been no godly influence? Besides the needless deaths of these pseudo-advisors, we would have been robbed of some of the most helpful end time information in scripture. The dream is recorded in Daniel, chapter two.

> *You, O king, were watching; and behold, a great image! This great image, whose splendor was excellent, stood before you; and its form was awesome. (32) This image's head was of fine gold, its chest and arms of silver, its belly and thighs of bronze, (33) its legs of iron, its feet partly of iron and partly of clay. (34) You watched while a stone was cut out without hands, which struck the image on its feet of iron and clay, and broke them in pieces. (35) Then the iron, the clay, the bronze, the silver, and the gold were crushed together, and became like chaff from*

> *the summer threshing floors; the wind*
> *carried them away so that no trace of them*
> *was found. And the stone that struck the*
> *image became a great mountain and filled*
> *the whole earth*
> *(Dan.2:31-35)*

Even given this information, it would have been a serious challenge to make sense of the dream. Daniel made it known to the king from the beginning that this dream was given to him by God and only God was wise enough to solve it.

> *This is the dream. Now we will tell the*
> *interpretation of it before the king. (37) You,*
> *O king, are a king of kings. For the God of*
> *heaven has given you a kingdom, power,*
> *strength, and glory; (38) and wherever the*
> *children of men dwell, or the beasts of the*
> *field and the birds of the heaven, He has*
> *given them into your hand, and has made*
> *you ruler over them all -- you are this head*
> *of gold. (39) But after you shall arise another*
> *kingdom inferior to yours; then another, a*
> *third kingdom of bronze, which shall rule*
> *over all the earth. (40) And the **fourth***
> ***kingdom**_shall be as strong as iron,*
> *inasmuch as iron breaks in pieces and*
> *shatters everything; and like iron that*
> *crushes, **that kingdom will break in pieces***
> ***and crush all the others**. (41) Whereas you*
> *saw the feet and toes, partly of potter's clay*
> *and partly of iron, the kingdom shall be*

divided; yet the strength of the iron shall be in it, just as you saw the iron mixed with ceramic clay. (42) And as the toes of the feet were partly of iron and partly of clay, so the kingdom shall be partly strong and partly fragile. (43) As you saw iron mixed with ceramic clay, they will mingle with the seed of men; but they will not adhere to one another, just as iron does not mix with clay. (44) And in the days of these kings the God of heaven will set up a kingdom which shall never be destroyed; and the kingdom shall not be left to other people; it shall break in pieces and consume all these kingdoms, and it shall stand forever. (45) Inasmuch as you saw that the stone was cut out of the mountain without hands, and that it broke in pieces the iron, the bronze, the clay, the silver, and the gold -- the great God has made known to the king what will come to pass after this. The dream is certain, and its interpretation is sure
(Dan. 2:36-45)

The Tale of Five Kingdoms

This dream could easily be titled "The Tale of Five Kingdoms". There are a few details about this dream that are very important for us to grasp. First, the dream covers an enormous span of time, from Daniel's day into the Kingdom Age, which is eternal in scope. Put another way, the king's dream went from one time zone to a completely different time zone. Second, four of the kingdoms were natural kingdoms; the fifth was a supernatural kingdom. Third, the four natural kingdoms had points where they began and ended, the fifth kingdom had a starting point but no ending point. Forth, notice that as you move from top to bottom (head to toe), the metals decrease in value, while increasing in hardness, which perhaps is evidence of the overall spiritual decline of the human race as implied in Genesis 4. From an historical/biblical overview, man started as a spiritual being, was placed in a perfect environment and will end in an apostate state giving allegiance to a demonized ruler while living in a defiled environment which has suffered under the wrath of God. Not a pretty picture. Fifth, after identifying the head as being Nebuchadnezzar's kingdom, very little time is spent on the second or third kingdom. Sixth, the kingdoms in Nebuchadnezzar's dream are generally agreed to be four world empires, these being Babylon, Medo-Persia, Greece and Rome. Seventh, more time is spent on the fourth kingdom than all the other preceding kingdoms combined. Eighth, the final kingdom has almost unanimous agreement among scholars that it represents the establishment of the Kingdom of God on earth. His Kingdom subdues and destroys all forms of unrighteousness and unfolds in two stages. First, the 1000-year reign known as the Millennial Reign of Christ (Rev. 20), and second, the New Jerusalem (Rev. 21) or the full manifestation of the eternal city.

Although Nebuchadnezzar's dream was a bit thin on details, this was intended to be a broad stroke overview and not a detailed accounting. In Daniel's latter years he would have encounters with God that would produce some of the most stunning details about the last days ever recorded in scripture. Chapters 7-12 contain the most complete verses, in terms of details and clarity about the last days, found anywhere in the Old Testament. These are rivaled only by their companion book, the Book of Revelation.

Please note that when King Nebuchadnezzar had his dream, none of the empires mentioned existed. Persia was simply another one of the provinces in Nebuchadnezzar's massive kingdom. Only wandering tribes occupied the Hellenistic states, later to become known as Greece. The city of Rome was an insignificant little town situated on the Tiber River. Who could have guessed that these locations were destined for such greatness? The wisdom of God is so awesome!

Daniel's Dream

We are now going to look at another supernatural download. This time however, the vision was given to Daniel directly. We are looking at this vision because it confirms the original dream given to Nebuchadnezzar and gives a startling view of last day events. John F. Walvoord, in his insightful commentary entitled, *"Daniel the Key to Prophetic Revelation" (p.145)*, states: *"In the interpretation of biblical prophecy, the seventh chapter of Daniel occupies a unique place. As interpreted by conservative expositors, the vision of Daniel provides the most comprehensive and detailed prophecy of future events to be found anywhere in the Old Testament. Although its interpretation has varied widely, conservative scholars generally are agreed, with few exceptions, that Daniel traces the course of four great world empires, namely, Babylon, Medo-Persia, Greece, and Rome, concluding in the climax of world history in the Second Coming of Jesus Christ and the inauguration of the eternal kingdom of God, represented as a fifth and final kingdom which is from heaven."*

Daniel 2 and 7 combine to give the most profound outline of future events in the entire Bible. Additional information is supplied later in Daniel's writings as well as numerous helpful references that are furnished by the New Testament's Book of Revelation. This information was given to the *Last Day Church* to help its people prepare their hearts for the coming firestorm. Sadly, few in today's church appear to take these prophetic lifelines to heart. These visions and dreams were not given simply to stimulate our intellectual curiosity, but were intended to provide God's people with critical end time insight. Those who take the revelation contained in these verses lightly may do so at the peril of their own soul (Matt.24:10).

Walvoord goes on to say that, "Chapter 7 views world history from God's standpoint in its immorality, brutality, and depravity. In terms of details, chapter 7 far exceeds chapter 2 and is in some sense the commentary on the earlier revelation" (p.151).

As we take a look at some of the passages in Daniel 7, please keep in mind that we are looking at things from an historical overview. Like the golf tournaments that feature a preview of the holes to be played by taking the viewers on a high-tech aerial recon. This is where we are going with this brief synopsis. We will make use of upcoming chapters to look at these events in greater detail.

The Four Beasts and the Coming Kingdom

In Daniel's vision he saw a great sea. Out of the sea began to emerge four beasts. The first three beasts are described in graphic detail and are agreed to represent the same three kingdoms as Daniel 2, Babylon, Medo-Persia and Greece. However, as was the case in chapter 2, the fourth beast captures Daniel's attention in a most unusual way. Again, more information is recorded about this kingdom (beast) than all the others combined. Let's look at the two sections of scripture that give us insight as to why Daniel was so intrigued by this particular beast.

> *After this I saw in the night visions, and behold, a fourth beast, dreadful and terrible, exceedingly strong. It had huge iron teeth; it was devouring, breaking in pieces, and trampling the residue with its feet. It was different from all the beasts that were before it, and it had ten horns. (8) I was considering the horns, and there was another horn, a little one, coming up among them, before whom three of the first horns were plucked out by the roots. And there, in this horn, were eyes like the eyes of a man, and a mouth speaking pompous words*
> *(Dan.7:7-8)*

> *I watched then because of the sound of the pompous words which the horn was speaking; I watched till the beast was slain, and its body destroyed and given to the burning flame. (12) As for the rest of the beasts, they had their dominion taken away, yet their lives were prolonged for a season and a time*
> *(Dan.7:11-12)*

What makes these particular verses so curious are the verses immediately following, namely, verse 13 and 14.

> *I was watching in the night visions, and*
> *behold, one like the Son of Man [Jesus],*
> *coming with the clouds of heaven! He came*
> *to the Ancient of Days [the Father], and they*
> *brought Him near before Him. (14) Then to*
> *Him [Jesus] was given dominion and glory*
> *and a kingdom that all peoples, nations, and*
> *languages should serve Him. His [Jesus]*
> *dominion is an everlasting dominion which*
> *shall not pass away [eternal in scope], and*
> *His kingdom the one which shall not be*
> *destroyed*
> *(Dan. 7:13-14)*

The Holy Spirit intentionally connects the description of the destruction of this fourth beast with the Second Coming of Christ. There is no mention of the destruction of the other three beasts, so there is a strong possibility that these empires continue to exist in some diminished state. In the last days, they simply are not as dominate as they were previously. It is clear that at the end of the current age the fourth beast will be destroyed and a heavenly kingdom will be established in its place (Rev.19:19-20).

By the way, Jewish scholars have always believed this to be true. Currently, in fact, they are anticipating Messiah to come, rebuild the temple in Jerusalem and establish His everlasting kingdom on earth. The only puzzle piece they are missing is His first advent, which of course is critical. God has a well-thought-out plan to remedy that problem.

Since we are planning to spend a great deal of time later in this book discussing the awesome revelation surrounding the future Millennial Reign of Christ, we will only lightly touch this subject now. When was the last time you heard a sermon on the Millennial Reign of Jesus Christ? Prepare your heart to be deeply impacted.

These verses (7-8; 11-14) are obviously speaking of the last days and the Second Coming of Christ. The Apostle John makes it clear that the antichrist is coming at the end of the age and that the church needs to be alert (1 Jn.2:18).

Back to the Future!

A good question at this juncture would be, "Why would Daniel's vision start with three beasts that are clearly represented and identified as being historical empires, then suddenly take a quantum leap into the future?"

Prophetic scriptures do that sometimes. For example, in Isaiah 61:1-2, the first and Second Comings of Christ are spoken of in one breath. For this reason, a number of prominent Jewish Rabbis have theorized that there were possibly two Messiahs. They could not imagine two separate comings, so they surmised that the Messiah pictured in Isaiah 53, the suffering servant, could not possibly be the strong and mighty deliverer of Isaiah 63. They found these two radically different caricatures of Messiah impossible to synchronize. Hence, the two-Messiah theory was born.

Prophetic scriptures often have multiple fulfillments. They are sometimes fulfilled in the life of the prophet or shortly thereafter and also have a future fulfillment. A few even have an ultimate fulfillment in the age to come. For example, take the event that the Bible calls the *"abomination of desolation"* (Dan.11:31; 12:11; Matt.24:15; Mk. 13:14). Historically, this has already been fulfilled twice. This first occurred in the Second Century B.C., when Antiochus Epiphanes defiled the Jewish Temple. Later in 70 A.D., a similar act was committed by the Roman General Titus. However, Jesus clearly applied Daniel's prophetic vision of this horrific act of wickedness to events shortly preceding His second appearing. There is still one more fulfillment and it will set off a chain of events that human beings living on this planet will never forget. The individual who is soon to appear on the world stage will make Adolf Hitler look like an amateur. This individual is identified by Daniel as the *"little horn"* that was speaking pompous words (Dan.7:8, 11, 20), and is the same one who continues to speak blasphemies in 2 Thess.2:3-4 and Rev.13:6.

Storm Watch

Most of today's Christians, when they hear this preached or read it in their Bibles, make absolutely no connection with the reality that these events will be played out in the very near future. Have you noticed that people seem to be so wrapped up in guessing when the Social Security Fund will finally be depleted that they miss the big picture? Beloved, the Bible calls such short sightedness, *"Straining at gnats while swallowing camels"* (Matt.23:24). When the end time events predicted in scripture begin to materialize, financial solvency will be the last thing on anyone's mind. When your pastor is publicly executed or the loving Christian family living next door is rounded up and strangers are placed in their home, what I am sharing will all make perfectly good sense. Jesus wants His people to know with certainty that what Daniel prophesied in Dan.12:1 was neither fiction nor the product of some "doom and gloom naysayer." Instead, it is a sure word of biblical prophecy and fully endorsed by the Son of God Himself (Matt. 24:21-22). Although we are probably several decades away from these horrendous events happening, please keep in mind that you don't build an ark when it's raining but while it's still relatively peaceful. Storm clouds are gathering on the not so distant horizon, and I pray you will see the wisdom of searching the scriptures daily to discover God's hidden wisdom for the coming hour when no one can work (Jn.9:4). We will discover that God has a wonderful plan for those who love Him with all their hearts. His people have nothing to fear as the time grows near. In fact, the church's most glorious days are still in the future. He has purposely preserved the best wine until the end (Jn.2:10). His promise to His purified bride is, *"Eye has not seen, nor ear heard, nor have entered into the heart of man, the things which God has prepared for those who love Him"* (1 Cor.2:9). This has both an end of the age fulfillment and will certainly be experienced in its fullness in the age to come.

CHAPTER 6

The Coming Storm

At that time Michael shall stand up, the great prince who stands watch over the sons of your people; and there shall be a time of trouble, such as never was since there was a nation, even to that time
(Dan.12:1)

There will be great tribulation, such as has not been since the beginning of the world until this time, no, nor ever shall be. (22) And unless those days were shortened no flesh would be saved; but for the elect's sake those days will be shortened
(Matt.24:21-22)

These are two of the most sobering verses in the Bible. Even more ominous is the reality that these verses will be fulfilled sooner than most imagine. Although we could still be several decades away from these verses impacting the planet, make no mistake about it, we are rushing towards a swift and catastrophic conclusion to the end of the age. If you are not directly effected, most likely your children will be and for sure your grandchildren will be. The Holy Spirit has communicated vital information to God's people through numerous end time prophetic words. It appears that very few today are taking these warnings seriously.

After Daniel gave King Nebuchadnezzar the interpretation to his stunning last day dream he concluded his statements by saying, *"The dream is certain, and its interpretation is sure"* (Dan.2:45b). The chilling events Daniel saw and described are non-negotiable from heaven's perspective.

While writing part of this book, my wife and I were in Florida, taking care of her ailing father. Hurricane Dennis, the strongest hurricane ever recorded this early in the season (a strong category three) slammed into Pensacola Beach in the Florida panhandle. The clearest signs that announce an approaching hurricane are the outer rain bands accompanied by unusually strong winds. These are felt hours ahead of the advancing storm and serve as nature's final notice that great danger is approaching.

What will soon be heading towards the nations of the earth is far worse than any killer hurricane. The events that will soon be taking place on a global scale are unprecedented in human history. Jesus made it clear that if God did not limit both the scope and shorten the duration of these cataclysmic events, there would be absolutely no survivors.

The Beginning of Sorrows

However, just as hurricanes have signs that telegraph their approaching threat, even so, Jesus calls the signs that foretell such tragic events, *"birth pangs"* or the *"beginning of sorrows"* (Rom.8:22; Matt.24:4). These are advance notices that His plan to shake the earth (Hag.2:6-7; Isa.2:19) is about to commence. The intensification of particular global happenings is the equivalent of the outer rain bands of a tropical depression or an impending hurricane. Let the reader be forewarned.

> *Now as He sat on the Mount of Olives, the disciples came to Him privately, saying, "Tell us, when will these things be? And what will be the sign of Your coming, and of the end of the age?" (4) And Jesus answered and said to them: "Take heed that no one deceives you. (5) For many will come in My name, saying, 'I am the Christ,' and will deceive many. (6) And you will hear of wars and rumors of wars. See that you are not troubled; for all these things must come to pass, but the end is not yet. (7) For nation will rise against nation, and kingdom against kingdom. And there will be famines, pestilences, and earthquakes in various places. (8)* **All these are the beginning of sorrows**
> *(Matt. 24:3-8)*

The disciples asked a two-fold question concerning the last days: when and what. Although Jesus never answers the *"when"* part of the question directly, by answering the *"what"* part of the question, one can do the math and have a pretty clear understanding of the timing dynamics.

The specific circumstances that comprise this time of sorrow are: (1) spiritual deception (2) break out of wars in numerous places (3) troubled spirit (unbelieving heart or a heart that is focused on negative events) (4) supernatural battles and interference (5) global starvation (6) outbreaks of numerous plagues and deadly diseases (7) Earthquakes and (8) tsunamis (implied - as these are the natural by-products of some of the larger earthquakes).

As we see these increase in both frequency and intensity, let the wise be discerning of the time. Our scientific approach to everything causes men to rely on man's wisdom more than on the Word of the Lord. Everything that God is releasing is intended to press men into taking a comprehensive spiritual inventory, thus causing them to turn and repent. Many will miss the supernatural source of these plagues because of the increase of scientific data and computerized diagnosis. Men will lean on technology to explain these bizarre events, rather than seeing the obvious objective, which is to humble man and cause him to seek the author of these calamities.

I take the events that Jesus defined literally. However, I by no means confine or limit the scope of events to simply those which Jesus specified. For instance, Jesus made it clear that there would be an increase both in the frequency and intensity of earthquakes. Earthquakes can generate a chain of events that produce many other destructive side effects. Besides the loss of life, there are massive financial consequences that are incurred from insurance claims, loss of jobs, emergency services, recovery and rebuilding costs, as well as a lack of productivity. If the earthquake were to take place in the ocean, then a tsunami could result that could decimate an entire region, as happened in the December 2004 tsunami in Indonesia. In addition to all the things we mentioned, there is always the threat of disease breaking out that can in some circumstances claim as many victims as the tsunami itself.

Secondary Causes

Secondary causes which result from catastrophic events are often more devastating than the actual events themselves. For instance, the most destructive feature associated with killer hurricanes is not created by the strong winds that these systems produce. Rather, it is a well-known fact that more lives are taken in the aftermath of these storms by flash floods resulting from the unusual rain amounts that these storms produce.

Another historical example of great devastation after a storm occurred shortly after the turn of the last century. During *"The Great San Francisco Earthquake of 1906"*, there was much greater loss of life and property after the quake from fire damage, than occurred during the earthquake itself.

Because of this, I believe the net impact of the impending disasters predicted by Jesus will be much larger than most are anticipating. Just as I could never have projected the far-reaching effects of the events that took place on 9/11, I believe the circumstances which Jesus identified as being part of the *"birth pangs"* or *"beginning of sorrows"* will alter business as usual on our planet and serve to set the stage for the brewing storm that will surely ensue. As troubling as these events will be in terms of loss of life, financial hardships, life disruption, etc., these events will seem insignificant when the tribulation period begins and God starts to release the twenty-one numbered judgments as described in the Book of Revelation.

Please always keep in mind that the ferocity of the catastrophic events that will be unleashed by God during the tribulation period are not designed to simply impress man with God's ability to create havoc in His universe whenever He so desires. Rather, it is the passionate response of a loving God who is willing to enact extreme measures in order to gain the attention and hopefully, the heart of a world that is spinning out of control. The God who *"so loved the world that He gave His only Son"* (Jn.3:16) to be brutally sacrificed upon a cross in order to save us hasn't changed His mind. In fact, the darker a man's heart seems to grow, the more creative and determined God appears to become in order to reach him.

Being able to make accurate assessments of the last day judgments just might make the difference in the temperature of your love. Those who misinterpret God's end time plans, will end up bitter and become cold-hearted (Matt. 24:12). Those who are discerning and have confidence in His plans will possess hearts that are on fire (Rev.3:15-16). The temperature of your love will be a matter of great importance in the days to come. The cold and fainthearted will become offended and will depart from the faith (1 Tim.4:1), ending up deceived and demonized. However, those full of the Holy Spirit and who have burning hearts for the Son of God, will grow strong and do great exploits (Dan.11:32).

The Offense Factor

One of the great weaknesses in the Body of Christ today is offense. Jesus warned those living in His day to guard against becoming offended (Matt.18:7). Offense leads to a defiled spirit and a defiled spirit is an open door for demonic activity. The Holy Spirit is training us now so we will be able to stand unoffended in the future.

*If you have run with the footmen, and they
have wearied you, then how can you contend
with horses? And if in the land of peace, in
which you trusted, they wearied you, then
how will you do in the floodplain of the
Jordan?*
(Jer.12:5)

We are currently attending the School of the Holy
Spirit. He is training us for our kingdom work assignments
(1 Cor.6:3). Learning obedience now is absolutely essential.
Faithfulness in small matters carries serious weight with
God. God promotes those who are both hearers and doers
of His Word (Jn.14:21). When we yield to an offense and
allow self-gratification to rule our lives, we disqualify
ourselves from being used effectively by God. Offenses
that are not addressed are fertile soil for strongholds to take
root. Strongholds are acquired and fortified by repeated
actions of disobedience. These repeated acts become like
the individual strands of a rope that have been braided
together. The more frequent the sin, the greater the strength
of the stronghold. Soon the stronghold has a strong hold on
your soul.

Strongholds are broken and overcome by the same
process that produces them. You develop strongholds by
repeated acts of disobedience and you break their power by
repeated acts of deliberate submission to the will of God.
Mike Bickle calls this, *"acting in the opposite spirit."* First
we repent (change our mind), then we turn and act in the
opposite spirit. If we have a problem with lying, when
faced with the opportunity to give a dishonest answer, we
intentionally tell the truth. That simple act of obedience
breaks one of those strands and the rope that binds us

weakens. So we get out of the hole the same way we got in; one shovelful at a time.

The same is true when it comes to overcoming offenses. Unresolved offenses lead to a bitter spirit. They defile not only the person who is carrying the offense but those around them (Heb.12:15). According to scripture, bitterness (accumulated unresolved offenses) is like being both poisoned and bound (Acts 8:23). This means that we are operating out of a defiled spirit (poisoned), and are spiritually handicapped (bound) from producing or reaching our full potential in God.

The Resisters

There will be a flood of Christians who will fall prey to an offended spirit in the last days (Matt.24:10) and it will cause their hearts to become cold. Rather than being the loving people that God desires, they will desert the church and their once tender hearts will become cesspools filled with bitter hatred. They will resist God and despise His church. Many will gather with other offended former Believers and lash out at those who are walking in righteousness. Some will even be directly responsible for others being martyred. These are spiritual Demas' (2 Tim.4:10) who like Paul's former friend (Philemon 24) deserted him and the faith because of secret attachments to worldly ambitions and carnal desires.

The coming storm is not for the faint, neither is it for the unprepared. The Holy Spirit has impressed me to write this book in order to call His people to a higher realm of consecration. Please understand that this warning is first addressing issues in my own life. Please do not for a moment interpret what I am writing as coming from one who has arrived. Not only have I not arrived, the longer I continue this journey, the less sure I am of what this trip is all about. As soon as I begin to think I have a clue, He shows up and reveals a whole new dimension of His kingdom and I feel like a spiritual toddler all over again.

CHAPTER 7

The Emerging World Dictator

Most Believers are familiar with the stories about an emerging world leader who will be the personification of evil. Although intrigued by these accounts, few take time to study this out, primarily because they believe they will be removed just prior to this wicked man's arrival. Therefore, they lack incentive to look into these matters in a serious way.

Besides the Messiah, the Bible gives more prophetic information about this man than any other person who has ever lived. There are good reasons for this. Sadly, most Christians I know are criminally ignorant about some of the significant details that God has shared in His Word for the purpose of preparing His people for the coming storm.

Even though this man's reign of terror will be extremely limited in time (Matt. 24:22) the devastation and carnage that will be left in his wake will be unparalleled in human history. Why should this matter? Hasn't every generation of Believers thought they would be facing this same end time scenario and it proved untrue? Why should our generation be any different?

Although I do not want to get side-tracked, let me give you four decisive reasons why our generation has more tangible evidence to bolster confidence that the events of the Book of Revelation will be played out in our lifetime. First is the global economy. The Antichrist's influence and control of large economic institutions will give him the power base necessary to assert many of his innovative social, economic and military reforms. Secondly is the advancement of global technologies. Until the recent establishment and deployment of advanced communications systems, many events in the Book of Revelation were inconceivable (Rev.11:9,11-13). Thirdly is the establishment of the State of Israel. Israel's restoration as a nation after nearly 2,000 years of her land lying dormant and her people scattered throughout the nations of the earth, rates as one of the great miracles of the Bible. Fourthly is the formation of the United Nations and the growing influence this organization exerts over the nations of the earth. I believe this organization's power and authority will continue to escalate and will provide much needed assistance to the Antichrist's regime. He will manipulate this organization to serve his own purposes. This will enable the Antichrist to establish his global decrees and give him access to the military resources that will permit him to enforce international mandates. No generation prior to ours has had all four of these key elements functioning on a global scale. Without these, the coming world dictator would be totally ineffective and could only impact a small region of the world.

I therefore conclude that there are several key last day events which absolutely could never have been fulfilled unless some of the scientific, political, economic and geographic breakthroughs of the past fifty years were in place. This mounting evidence gives testimony to the uniqueness of the generation in which we are living.

Last Day Training Manual

I want our generation to start looking at Bible prophecy as a living reality rather than as an intellectual curiosity. Many are drawn to end time subjects simply out of intrigue. These are the kind of people who find pleasure solving difficult crossword puzzles or forensic scientists who gain satisfaction from discovering a critical clue that could shed new light on a criminal investigation. Some approach Bible prophecy with that kind of academic inquisitiveness.

We need to study end time prophetic verses of scripture as God's last day training manual. In order to train for a mission, you must first have accurate information of the circumstances you will be facing. Otherwise, all your time, energy and training may turn out to be a waste of time.

When I was sent to Vietnam, ninety-five percent of our training was with conventional warfare tactics. The problem with this type of training was that we weren't fighting a conventional war. Vietnam was fought in a jungle environment and required a totally different strategic skill set. My tactical training did little to prepare me for those circumstances.

God has provided His people with a brilliant training manual that describes in great detail what the enemy will be doing and what we can do to have the greatest impact. The problem is that most Believers are convinced that: (1) the training manual is either irrelevant and contains no practical assistance (2) is symbolic and needs not be taken literally (3) is unnecessary as the troops will be removed before the fighting begins or that (4) the manual is too complicated and the job of interpreting it must be left exclusively to the West Point graduates.

I feel like that voice crying in the wilderness, *"Prepare the way of the Lord"* (Matt.11:10). I have learned that people rarely prepare for circumstances they do not anticipate will happen. Also, we prepare according to the degree of difficulty we expect to encounter. People who are expecting to face the eye wall of a category five hurricane prepare in an entirely different way than those who are expecting to receive gale force winds.

The end time events that are described in stunning clarity and could possibly unfold in the lives of your children and grandchildren are intended to be taken seriously. Although you can do little to avoid these catastrophic occurrences, you can gain insight and offer instruction to those you care about. Do you really think God would dedicate over a hundred chapters of scripture to a subject that is optional reading or that were written exclusively for the bright and gifted?

The Tribulation Begins

Many Christians miss the fact that the period commonly referred to as the Tribulation Period is an event that is broken up into two distinct time periods. I believe that it is essential to point this out because these two periods will vary greatly in both strategy and intensity. The Tribulation Period is a seven year period that is split into two equal time spans that are forty-two months (three and a half years) in duration. For the sake of clarity I will refer to the first half of the Tribulation Period simply as the Tribulation. I will refer to the second half of the Tribulation Period as the Great Tribulation (Matt.24:21).

This Tribulation Period is preceded by a time known as the *"beginning of sorrows"* (Mk.13:8). This is like the proverbial plow shaft that turns the soil in order to prepare it for the seed that will shortly be sown. This season of time will be paving the way for the evil world dictator who is soon to arrive. During this same period of time, pressure will be brought to bear on every human institution known to man. The name, *"beginning of sorrows,"* identifies the impact that this turbulent period will have on the whole earth. The stress that will be placed upon governments to meet the escalating global crises will be absolutely astounding. Governmental, economic, social, religious, ecological, technological and military structures will be stretched to their limits in order to keep pace with the collapsing infrastructure. I am personally convinced that we are at the very beginning of this cycle and there is nothing any of us can do to stop the sequence of events that are coming.

As chilling as that last statement may appear, I do believe that God is purposely establishing a *"grass-roots-last-day"* prayer movement which will have a profound impact on these events (Isa.62:1,6). "How can a prayer movement have an impact on events that are clearly prophesied in God's Word? After all, isn't His Word unchangeable," someone might ask?

> *So I sought for a man among them who would make a wall, and stand in the gap before Me on behalf of the land, that I should not destroy it; but I found no one (Ezek.22:30)*

The absence of committed intercessors limits what God is willing to do. Just because God specifies that certain things will occur does not mean that these cannot be altered in scope or intensity by prayer. I want to be clear that I am referring to minimizing not eliminating. These events surely will take place as written; however, prayer can clearly affect the way they are played out.

With that in mind, there are two things I would like you to consider when it comes to this matter of intercession. First, God wrote this knowing full well that a strong prayer movement would be established in the last days. Although these events will certainly take place, they will be performed with the minimum amount of force necessary to produce a maximum number of conversions. Prayer can soften even the worst of tragedies.

Secondly, because of the fervent prayers that have been offered on behalf of those suffering under the weight of God's wrath, God will release pockets of mercy. These will be places where God will pass over, just like He did in Goshen to protect His people while living in Egypt. Without the prayer movement however, the same results would follow as described in the above scripture (Ez.22:30). When the twenty-one numbered judgments are released, they will impact billions of people globally. Simultaneously, the prayer movement will be impacting millions, which is not an inconsequential number and is currently worthy of full consideration.

I like to think of intercessory prayer as God's air force. A strong air force is essential for total effectiveness during a military campaign. As the wicked world dictator attempts to exert his great military influence and crush every pocket of resistance, God's air force (strategic prayer networks) will be a counter measure that will both alter, minimize and in some cases counteract some of his most diabolical schemes (Matt.7:7).

When this leader appears on the world stage, he will have a way about him that will mesmerize entire nations. He will come on the scene at a time of unprecedented international confusion and disruption. Leaders of countries will be scrambling to maintain a sense of order, as anarchy will be prevalent and spreading rapidly. His calm demeanor will be in stark contrast to the stressed-out world from which he emerges. His grasp of critical issues will captivate the masses and his common sense approach to remedying these problems will win him great fame and international popularity (Dan.11:21). He will be seen nightly on the numerous satellite news broadcasts and his wisdom will silence even his worst critics. He will be known as a man who desires to bring global peace and will appear to reach out and embrace a pluralistic society.

Behind the scenes he will be building a secret network of alliances that will become visible at a crucial point in his administration. His charm and charisma will make even staunch adversaries take notice. One of his most challenging tasks will be to negotiate a stunning peace agreement in the Middle East (Dan.9:27). His sweeping success at being able to negotiate *"unheard of"* terms between warring factions within the Muslim community will further serve to gain him international notoriety. He will be the talk of the nations. The Bible says he will acquire his position and power by *"intrigue"* (Dan.11:21).

The most stunning of all his accomplishments will be the peace treaty that he negotiates between Israel and the Muslim world that will enable Israel to rebuild the Tribulation Temple on the same site where both their previous temples stood (Dan.9:26-27). This announcement will stun the nations of the earth and will cause their allegiance to him to be significantly strengthened. Few will recognize his true intentions for they will not surface until after the Jewish temple has been constructed and is in full operation.

The Unholy Trinity

One of the things that helps enhance the visibility of this emerging world leader is a person whom the Bible identifies as the *"false prophet"* (Rev.19:20). Just as the world dictator will be the key political figure during the Tribulation Period, this individual will be the primary spiritual leader during this same span of time. Working behind the scenes and giving these two puppets supernatural power will be none other than Satan himself (Rev.12:9,12). These three will make up what can best be described as a counterfeit trinity. Their unholy alliance will prove to be the most deadly coalition ever assembled in the history of mankind. Before they are stripped of their power and authority by God (Dan.9:24) billions of people will be deceived and suffer unimaginable losses (Matt.24:21-24).

One of the bizarre events that takes place during the beginning of the tribulation is the fatal head wound that the world dictator will suffer (Rev.13:3). Most likely the wound will be caused by an assassin who will inflict the deadly wound with a large knife or sword (Rev.13:14). This will be headline news and will spread across the globe in a flash. The entire earth will mourn because they believed in the unlimited potential in this brilliant new leader. Then suddenly the false prophet, empowered by Satan himself (Rev.13:2) will create an enormous public stir by bringing this political figure back to life. It will have the same dramatic effect as if someone had raised President Kennedy from the dead.

The impact of this dramatic resurrection will be that this rising political dictator will have astonished the entire world. This will instantly elevate his political career to heights that were formerly unthinkable. He will have the popularity and status of an international rock star, actor and athlete all rolled into one. The world will be eating out of his hands. Television cameras will follow his every move and interviews of his dramatic story will be played twenty-four hours a day. The entire planet will be repeating his story in every conceivable language and setting.

His skyrocketing popularity will cause most of the world to believe that this leader has immortal qualities. The false prophet will encourage this myth and satanic worship will be the outcome (Rev.13:4). There will be a growing consensus that this leader is absolutely invincible. To reinforce this, a huge image will be erected in his honor and the world will stand speechless as the false prophet, through counterfeit signs and wonders, enables this statue to speak (2 Thess.2:9). It will decree that the world dictator should be worshipped as God and that anyone refusing to do so should be put to death (Rev.13:15). This will instantly put true Believers at risk and many will face martyrdom (Rev.13:7). For them, denying Christ will not be an option.

The Mark of the Beast

The false prophet will have the power to call down fire from heaven and do an assortment of supernatural feats that will leave people totally astonished and completely captivated (Rev.13:13). He will also be the mastermind behind what the Bible refers to as *"the mark of the beast"* (Rev.13:16). He will devise an elaborate computerized system that will undoubtedly gain international acceptance through the endorsement of the expanded powers given to the United Nations. This will be heralded as a brilliant commercial breakthrough. Under this mandate only those who have received a mark on their right hand or forehead will be able to purchase or sell goods (Rev.13:16-17). This will eliminate the use of various currencies and will quickly gain international acceptance. Anyone refusing this mark will be unable to purchase basic essentials such as food, clothing or shelter. Neither will they be able to work or receive compensation as all assets will be funneled through this global economic system.

This will be a key strategic move as it will set in place a global financial network and give the political leader a whole new level of international credibility and governmental supremacy. This will also pave the way for his next venture which is universal military domination. This political leader's plan is to eventually be in complete control of the four key spheres of life: economic, political (governmental), military and religious. If he can accomplish this, he will have no problem establishing himself as the uncontested leader of global affairs. His word will be law and anyone who dares to oppose him will be eliminated immediately.

During the first forty-two months of the Tribulation Period, this political figure will be scrambling to consolidate his power base and establish himself as the new leader of the emerging one-world government. His growing popularity will be so universal that anyone not giving their full allegiance to him will be considered a threat to global peace and security (1 Thess.5:3).

The Resisters

The strongest form of resistance will come from two very different groups. The first will be the end time church. Believers will be given a strong spirit of revelation and will quickly discern what this diabolical duo is up to. They will understand that these two conspirators are clearly the ones identified in scripture as the two beasts (Rev.13:1,2,11) and that they are controlled by none other than Satan himself (Rev.13:2). When they refuse to comply with the universal decree to receive the beast's mark they will be hated, hunted and when found, beheaded (Rev.20:4).

The political leader is identified in scripture as *"the Antichrist"* (1 Jn.2:18). Other titles given to him are *"the man of sin"* (2 Thess.2:3), *"the lawless one"* (2 Thess.2:8, 9), *"the son of perdition"* (2 Thess.2:3) and *"the beast"* (Rev.13:2).

The other group, the resisters, will be equally noncompliant, but for very different reasons. Although it is difficult to find hard biblical verification to make a strong case, history is rich with examples of those who refused to yield their allegiance to ruthless dictators. The French resistance is one such example. Although well aware of the fatal consequences if discovered, tens of thousands of French citizens chose to resist Hitler's oppressive reign and face death rather than yield and subjugate themselves to his tactics of fear and intimidation.

Resisters are scattered throughout history and have consistently opposed evil dictatorships. Millions have suffered execution and other forms of public humiliation rather then submit to the whims of wicked rulers. Because resisters are so well documented historically, the burden of proof to substantiate that the Antichrist's reign of terror will break with historical precedent falls upon those who would suggest otherwise. In addition to historical precedent, even a casual reading of Daniel 11 makes it abundantly clear that there is much resistance and a growing dissatisfaction with the Antichrists' global leadership. This ends up consuming a great deal of his time and military resources.

These resisters will be individuals whom the Lord allows to see through the deception and they will loathe these two world leaders because they sense the evil motivation behind their sweeping reforms. Although their defiance has no religious affiliation, they deeply resent having to yield all their civil rights and privacy to the new global system. They would rather resist, even if it means enduring governmental harassment or death, than concede their personal freedoms. They will not be impressed by the talking image, the resurrected political figure, his spiritual guide or his lying signs and wonders (2 Thess.2:9). They are a hardy group of rugged individualists who strongly resent being manipulated by the system. They would rather flee and live off the land in small isolated groups than submit to tyranny. They will be misunderstood by some of their closest friends and family and will be considered outlaws. Because they refuse *"the mark of the Beast,"* many will be brought to true saving faith before the end of the age. Others will be allowed to enter Christ's Millennial Kingdom in their natural bodies. We will develop that train of thought in the section that deals with Jesus' Millennial reign on earth. Although these two groups will have completely different reasons that compel them to stand against the newly formed global government, they will be equally detested and sought out as political fugitives.

Most of these events will develop just prior to the last forty-two months or roughly three-and-a-half years before the Lord returns (1 Thess.4:16-17). This will also be the most horrific time that mankind has ever experienced (Matt.24:21-22) and will be known as *"The Great Tribulation" or "the time of Jacob's trouble"* (Matt.24:21; Jer.30:7). The church of Jesus Christ must be informed on these matters because we have been warned that many

Believers will become disillusioned and will even *"depart from the faith"* (1 Tim.4:1). I take no delight in having to make these kinds of statements as it causes my heart to grieve and my spirit to tremble.

Literary License

I realize that I have taken some literary license and embellished some of the end time text. I have done so to help the reader get an expanded view of the events that will soon be unfolding. There are such broad implications with some of these verses that I have simply tried to apply my sanctified imagination in order to fill in the blanks. I will attempt to take this approach throughout the remainder of this book as I believe the scripture encourages us to engage in such a discovery process and gives us permission to search out these prophetic enigmas (Pro.25:2; Dan.2:21-22). Because some of what you will be reading is highly subjective and open to interpretation, I encourage the reader to take time to pause and examine the scriptures that I have referenced (Acts 17:11). These are the verses upon which I am basing my conclusions. I hope you find these insights helpful.

CHAPTER 8

The Battle for Jerusalem

Without a clear understanding of the things we will be discussing in this chapter, the end times will never quite make sense. Many people, when approaching the events that are described in the last day accounts in scripture, get so absorbed in the details that they seem to lose sight of what is driving these bizarre events.

There will be a series of remarkable battles that will rage towards the end of the age as the forces of good and evil are assembled and clash in unprecedented fashion. This demonic campaign will be fought on numerous fronts and in many locations but will ultimately culminate in Israel. My guess, based on Rev.14:20, is that more people could possibly be killed in this series of battles than the sum total of combatants slain in all of military history. I realize the enormity of that statement. However, when you try to imagine what a two hundred mile tract of land would look like littered with dead bodies stacked about five feet high, whatever the final body count ends up being, surely it will be in the hundreds of millions. This is simply the number destroyed in the grand finale.

Satan's Eviction Notice

Prior to this epic end time battle there are multiple skirmishes being fought simultaneously in many nations during the final three-and-a-half years or the period commonly referred to as *The Great Tribulation*. Jesus underscored the tragic loss of human lives by stating, *"And unless those days were shortened, no flesh would be saved [survive]; but for the elect's [Believers'] sake those days will be shortened"* (Matt 24:22). Only the kindness and divine intervention of God will save mankind from total annihilation (Hab.3:2). Someone once said, *"Sin takes you places you really don't want to go; keeps you longer than you want to stay; and costs you more than you want to pay."* Sadly, this appears to be the final testimony of mankind.

Jesus gave His friend John a sneak preview of what will be happening behind the scenes that will cause things to escalate so rapidly.

> *And war broke out in heaven: Michael and his angels fought with the dragon [Satan]; and the dragon and his angels [demons] fought, (8) but they did not prevail, nor was a place found for them [Satan and his demonic host] in heaven any longer. (9) So the great dragon [Satan] was cast out, that serpent of old, called the Devil and Satan, who deceives the whole world;* **he was cast to the earth,** *and his angels [demons or fallen angels] were cast out with him*
> *(Rev.12:7-9)*

> *Therefore rejoice, O heavens, and you who dwell in them! Woe to the inhabitants of the earth and the sea!* **For the devil has come down to you, having great wrath, because he knows that he has a short time**
> *(Rev.12:12)*

Satan's eviction from heaven will evoke two completely different responses. Heaven will rejoice and the earth will soon be full of mourning. This eviction is a future event and is forecasted to take place during the Tribulation period.

One of the great theological questions of all time is, "How has God tolerated Satan's presence for such an extended period of time?" Trying to answer that baffling question is like trying to figure out what God was thinking when he created sharks. Raised near the ocean and spending much of my free time surfing, that question has great significance for me. I must admit that I am clueless on both accounts; however I have full assurance in my spirit that God has an awesome answer for both of those perplexing questions.

The Word of God is clear that Satan currently spends most of his time fulfilling his accusatory role (Rev.12:10), with which, by the way, he has become very proficient. We know this because: (1) he has been doing it for a very long time (2) he has been very successful at his profession and (3) because we continue to supply him with an abundance of material with which to accuse us.

There are four details that I want to make sure we do not miss: (1) Satan is coming down to earth (2) he is really angry (3) he has a real grasp of God's last day timetable and (4) his destruction will be swift. Therefore, he will be attempting to inflict maximum damage in the minimum amount of time that remains.

Satan's Incarceration

Why is this information important for us to know? What is it that has the devil so preoccupied that he can't think of anything else but annihilating every thing on the planet that breathes? These are really important questions for us to be asking at this stage in human history. The answer may not be as difficult as you might suppose.

In order to accurately respond, we must jump ahead in the story line and look at the twentieth chapter of the Book of Revelation. We will look at this critical chapter in much greater detail later, but there are a few insights that are important for us to grasp at this juncture.

> *Then I saw an angel coming down from heaven, having the key to the bottomless pit and a great chain in his hand. (2) He laid hold of the dragon, that serpent of old, who is the Devil and Satan, and bound him for a thousand years; (3) and he cast him into the bottomless pit, and shut him up, and set a seal on him, so that he should deceive the nations no more till the thousand years were finished. But after these things he must be released for a little while*
> *(Rev.20:1-3)*

> *Now when the thousand years have expired, Satan will be released from his prison (8) and will go out to deceive the nations which are in the four corners of the earth, Gog and Magog, to gather them together to battle, whose number is as the sand of the sea. (9) They went up on the breadth of the earth and surrounded the camp of the saints and the beloved city. And fire came down from God out of heaven and devoured them. (10) The*

devil, who deceived them, was cast into the
lake of fire and brimstone where the beast
and the false prophet are. And they will be
tormented day and night forever and ever
(Rev.20:7-10)

Satan's Secret Obsession

The thing that is weighing on Satan's mind is his impending prison sentence. He is well aware that God's prophetic Word declares that he will be spending 1,000 years bound up and thrown into the bottomless pit. Then he will be released or paroled for a very brief season and finally rearrested and incarcerated forever in the lake of fire where the torment never ceases. Whenever he thinks about this he is filled with rage and violent resolve to kill as many humans as possible. Why humans? Simply because they are made in God's image and because he knows how much God loves mankind. Whatever God loves, he hates, and whatever God hates (sin of any kind), Satan loves.

The Devil has looked at every means of escape possible in order to avoid his term of incarceration and anguish when at last he is sentenced to spend eternity in the lake of fire (Rev.20:2,10). His extensive search has yielded only one possible strategy which he believes will accomplish this task. Remember, he is frantic because his very survival is at stake. He is operating in a full-desperation mode. His pride has always caused him to believe that he can out-think God. Now is his moment of truth and he is thoroughly convinced that he has discovered the one loophole in God's Word that will enable him to save his skin. If he can pull it off, he will remain out on parole indefinitely. He is banking everything on his plan

103

succeeding. There is absolutely no Plan B in the works. He is well aware that this is a high stakes game of winner takes all. His very existence hinges on the accomplishment of this plan.

Unveiling a Great Mystery

Would you be interested to know exactly what that plan involves? I had a hunch you might. The plan involves exploiting a prophetic promise given 2,000 years ago by Jesus which was specifically addressed to the Jewish leadership.

> *O Jerusalem, Jerusalem, the one who kills the prophets and stones those who are sent to her! How often I wanted to gather your children together, as a hen gathers her chicks under her wings, but you were not willing! (38) See! Your house is left to you desolate; (39) for I say to you [Jewish leaders at the end of the age], you shall see Me no more [I refuse to come back] till you [Jewish leaders] say, Blessed is He who comes in the name of the LORD*
> *(Matt. 23:37-39)*

Focus on that last phrase for just a moment. I have added some points of clarification in the parentheses. Let's look at one more key verse, then we will put all these together and help you see what's happening.

> *Repent therefore and be converted, that your sins may be blotted out, so that times of*

refreshing may come from the presence of the Lord, (20) and that He [the Father] may send Jesus Christ, who was preached to you before, (21) whom heaven must receive [Jesus must remain in heaven] until the times of restoration of all things [the clear conditions established and spoken by the prophets], which God has spoken by the mouth of all His holy prophets (Acts 3:19-21)

Please stay with me on this important issue. Jesus Christ has bound Himself, by His Word, and has plainly stated that He will only return to earth when earnestly invited by a group of believing Jewish leaders who will petition Him from Jerusalem. Please understand two things: (1) the Gentile church cannot fulfill this Word by proxy and (2) this is the furthest thing from the mind of the average Jewish citizen living in Israel today. This presents quite a dilemma.

High Stakes

This Word (Matt.23:37) is a clear mandate and has been given exclusively to the Jewish people and will be fully activated at the end of the age. If you give serious consideration to the implications of what Jesus was prophesying here, I believe you will agree that the ramifications are staggering. Think about it. The entire end time scenario hinges on whether or not this verse is acted upon. Did you catch that? If the Jews don't cry out, Jesus doesn't return. Can you imagine anything more crucial to the plan of God and to our future destiny than this? Selah!

Jesus was well aware that the ancient Jews would reject Him. He was a major co-signer on the Isaiah 53 passages which were written over seven hundred years prior to His first coming. Although their lack of discernment grieved His heart (Matt. 16:3), He was not caught off-guard by their spiritual blindness.

Because *"His word is settled in heaven"* (Ps.119:89) and because He is *"Not a man that He should lie"* (Num.23:19), Jesus has bound Himself by His solemn oath. He has promised and will keep His promise, not to return to earth until His ancient people, the Jews, welcome Him home in a spirit of unison. Jesus knows that this will happen just as He prophesied.

However, if in any way He were to violate His Word, He would disqualify Himself as High Priest and thus nullify His atonement. Are you still with me? In the adversary's mind, that would be stalemate.

Someone might ask, "How could Jesus violate His Word and give opportunity to the adversary?" If there is no appeal from a unified Jewish people for Him to return and if Jesus were to decide to return anyway, that would be a huge breach of His Word. Even though on the one hand He would be fulfilling His promise to come back, on the other He would be violating His promise to return only after a unified cry came from the hearts of His people crying out from Jerusalem. Are you catching the gravity of this circumstance? This is no minor promise. This is our entire future-hope and security that is on the line here. The enemy is well aware of what is at stake and has a plan that he is confident will succeed and keep him out of prison. Would you be interested in knowing what that plan is? I thought so.

The promise that Jesus made involves both a specific place and a specific people. The place is Jerusalem and the people are the Jews. Therefore, there must be Jewish people living in their Jewish homeland. Why? Because Jerusalem is mentioned specifically in Jesus' prophetic promise, which is why God dispatched messengers from heaven and prophets to prophesy (Zech.14:14) His return to the Mount of Olives (Acts 1:9-11). Therefore, it is crucial that there be a Jewish people alive and living in the land of Israel.

Another Holocaust?

So, if there must be a born-again Jewish people alive and living in the land of Israel in order for Jesus to return, what must Satan do to ensure this never happens? He must set up a scenario that will effectively guarantee the wholesale annihilation of every Jewish man, woman and child that lives on the planet. As bizarre as that might seem to you, that is exactly what Satan plans to do. If you do not view the end times through that lens, you will never understand what's really happening behind the scenes. You can have a basic knowledge of every single last day event and still miss what's really driving Satan's anger.

Satan is more focused on his survival than he is on any other issue. He sees his ability to exist totally tied into the continuation and spiritual prosperity of the Jewish people. This, by the way, is not a new thought; he understood God's prophetic decree concerning his demise back in the garden (Gen.3:15). Since that time, his very existence has been his overriding concern. Self-preservation defines every move he makes. His entire being quivers with volcanic rage at the very thought of being confined for

1,000 years in the *"bottomless pit"* and he erupts with fury when he considers his ultimate incarceration in the *"lake of fire"* (Rev.20:3,10).

"Okay," you say, "that sounds pretty heavy, but what does that have to do with me and my family?" The answer is, "absolutely everything." Follow the logic. The key to Satan's plan to thwart the Second Coming of Jesus and thus stay out of prison (Rev.20:10) is contingent upon the absolute obliteration of the Jewish people. If that were to happen then all of God's end time plans and purposes would be suspended indefinitely. If there is no Second Coming (2 Tim.2:13) then there can be no resurrection from the dead (1 Cor.15:13), no glorified bodies (1 Cor.15:52), no Millennial Kingdom (Rev.20), no New Heaven and no New Earth (Rev.21:1).

Are you beginning to see the scope of things? Said more succinctly, if Satan's plan succeeds, your future destiny in God just got blown entirely off the map. Obviously, you would not still be reading if, for a moment, you thought his demonic plan had even the remotest possibility of success. I commend you for both your insight and perseverance while I developed this essential strategic point. There absolutely will be a fiery Jewish remnant alive and living in Jerusalem who will passionately cry out for Him to have mercy and return to His city (Ps. 48:2).

Is it beginning to become clearer why a nation the size of New Jersey located half way across the earth continues to dominate world news evening after evening? Even as you are reading this, nations are discussing, drafting and ratifying legislation which is defining their opposition to God's covenant people, Israel. Most will utterly abandon her as time progresses. Oil consumption and global influences are pressuring the nations of the earth to strengthen alliances that are mostly hostile in both their treatment of and their commitment to the Jewish people. They will ultimately do so to their own peril (Joel 3:2-3). God's timeless promise to bless those who bless Israel and to curse those who mistreat her (Gen.12:3) has never been rescinded. The nations would be wise to heed God's prophetic warning, *"I will make Jerusalem a very heavy stone for all peoples; all who would heave it away will surely be cut in pieces"* (Zech.12:3).

Satan's primary instrument to try to purge the earth of the Jewish people will be the Antichrist's ruthless regime. This is the subject of Revelation 12 and we will look at this chapter in detail later. What is important at this stage is that you have a strong grasp of what is going on *behind the scenes* which is producing the events that will be future newsmakers. Only a small fragment of the Body of Christ today has any idea about what is getting ready to break-in on the planet. In addition, few have understanding about what is really driving these events.

The Great Delusion

The primary spirit that will be released in great measure at the end of the age is a strong spirit of deception. This demonic spirit's assignment will be to convince people that evil things are good and that good things are evil (Isa.5:20). He will be extremely successful. Jesus always referred to this spirit when he spoke about the last days (Matt.24:4). This spirit is given access to people who compromise the integrity of God's Word. It always starts with a little compromise and grows into full rebellion if not quickly confronted and dealt with through sincere confession and repentance (Ja.5:16). These are the *"little foxes"* referred to in the Song of Solomon (2:15). They are mostly secret sins (Ps.90:8) that create pockets of darkness in our soul and give demonic spirits authority to harass and oppress. One of the most troubling verses in the New Testament that is clearly directed to the last day church was penned by the Apostle Paul to his young understudy, Timothy. The warning can only be misunderstood by those who are leaning away from the truth.

> *Now the Spirit expressly says [warns] that in latter times [last days] some [professing Believers] will **depart from the faith** [stop believing], giving heed to deceiving spirits and doctrines of demons [yield to a spirit of deception]*
> *(1 Tim.4:1)*

This should make the coldest heart begin to tremble. This admonition is directed to anyone in the Body of Christ who is flirting with areas of hidden sin and is currently deceived into believing that God's mercy is a sign of His lack of concern in these matters. I assure you that nothing could be further from the truth. Darkness always produces greater darkness. There is no neutral corner when it comes to sin issues. Sin begets sin. The seed of sin sown today will yield a harvest of unrighteousness tomorrow if not aggressively resisted and swiftly dealt with through confession and repentance (Pro.28:13). Jesus recommended aggressive action be taken to remove ourselves from any area that produces spiritual compromise (Matt. 5:28-30).

Sadly, many of God's people will have to deal with great regret when Jesus appears (1 Cor.3:13-15). They will suddenly become keenly aware of the amount of time, effort, money and unnecessary pain their sinful indulgences cost them. What they will forfeit in the coming age will grieve them to a degree that words are inadequate to describe. Missed opportunities to go deep in Christ, reach and impact lost friends and serve others in the Body of Christ will weigh on their hearts in a profound way. Paul coined the phrase *"to suffer loss"* (1 Cor.3:15) in order to describe and highlight the aftermath of missing out on clearly obtainable rewards. There will be a sense of loss and a realization of squandered resources.

Having said all that, I do not wish for you to misinterpret what I am attempting to communicate here. I am not even **slightly** implying that folks in the coming age will spend their time walking around with a spirit of condemnation or with a residue of heaviness because they are constantly ruminating over past shortcomings. Not only are there no Bible verses to support that line of thought, but it totally misrepresents the character and compassion of Jesus. Jesus' kindness will instantly remove and defuse any tendency to wallow in self-pity and regret. It will be impossible for any Believer to stand in His presence with a defiled (accusatory) spirit at that time in history. Additionally, there will be no time for evil spirits to harass anyone during that period anyway. Demons will find themselves a little preoccupied with the *"Lake of Fire"* and will probably spend their days irritating each other. They will find it extremely difficult to weep, gnash teeth and harass at the same time.

For those of you brave enough to continue, we will cover this subject extensively in the chapter entitled, *"The Future Judgments of God."* This chapter will surprise many in how encouraging and forgiving Jesus will be in handling our weak attempts to love Him.

CHAPTER 9

The Abomination of Desolation

Author's note:
I will be using a storyline format in this chapter. I believe this will be the most effective communication tool to bring clarity and simplicity to a subject that historically has been greatly overstated and often employs language and details that serve to confuse rather than inform. This format will require that I use creativity in order to fill in the blanks left silent in scripture.

I will be operating much like a forensic team which gathers small fragments of information and from those limited clues must make an educated guess at what actually took place. I will insert scripture references when appropriate so you can follow along with your Bible in hand. Let's get started.

> *They [the Antichrist and the false prophet] shall defile the sanctuary fortress [Tribulation Temple in Jerusalem]; then they **shall take away the daily sacrifices** [temple sacrificial system removed], and place there the abomination of desolation [the Antichrist will make blasphemous statements against God and promote lies about himself] (Dan.11:31)*

> *And from the time that the daily sacrifice is taken away [temple sacrifices cease], and*

the abomination of desolation is set up [the installation of Antichrist worship] (Dan.12:11)

Therefore when you see [will be broadcast via satellite across the entire earth] the abomination of desolation, spoken of by Daniel the prophet, standing in the holy place [whoever reads, let him understand], (16) then let those who are in Judea flee to the mountains [there is action required] (Matt.24:15-16)

*But when you see **Jerusalem surrounded by armies** [the Antichrist's military coalition], then know that its desolation is near (Luke 21:20)*

The episode called the *"Abomination of Desolation"* is one of the most repugnant events that will ever take place in human history. It will certainly be a low water mark that will be unrivaled in terms of its blatant public defiance of God. It will be a deliberate mass deception aimed at defiling His character and nature. The Antichrist will be unrelenting in his boasts of personal deity. Be forewarned, he will be extremely convincing and most of the planet will be swept up in his diabolical masquerade. The story and events could look something like this.

Since stepping into the international spotlight over three-and-a-half years ago, The Leader (the Antichrist) has been laboring behind the scenes to put together a coalition of nations that will form an evil alliance and will provide him the economic, military and political resources necessary to mount an extremely deceptive, yet incredibly effective, hostile global takeover (Dan.11:21,23). This move ultimately positions him for international notoriety and world dominance. He was promised this when he made his secret pact with none other than Satan himself (Dan.8:24). The price tag for his rise to power was merely the total relinquishing of all personal rights and full submission to Satan's end time scheme. In time, he will live to regret having ever entertained such notions.

He quickly gained the respect of many world leaders and stunned the entire world with the success of his shocking Middle East negotiations. These consultations between the Jews and their Arab neighbors produced unheard-of terms. For the first time since Israel's rebirth as a nation in 1948, real peace seemed to have been accomplished. His connections in the Arab world made it possible for him to secure the Temple Mount area. This put the world's most highly contested piece of real estate back under the sovereign control of the nation of Israel. This was the first time in over 2,000 years that the Jewish people had possessed such authority. Although the concessions Israel made to secure this area were extremely costly, both in terms of its economic impact and long term disarmament agreements, the benefits seemed to far outweigh the sacrifices. Israel gleefully signed the proposed covenant (Dan.9:27) in good faith. With the exception of a few troublesome Messianic Jewish leaders who persistently had given the Jews grave warnings, the agreement (Isa.28:15) was accepted and signed into law. After much celebration and international fanfare, and in accordance with the terms of the freshly-drafted covenant, the Muslim shrines that had occupied the Temple Mount area for the past 1,300 years, were painstakingly dismantled and moved to the agreed upon location in the newly recognized State of Palestine.

While Arab engineers worked on reassembling their holy shrines in Palestine, Jewish site preparation moved ahead with stunning coordination and speed. The site work seemed to be progressing so rapidly and with such flawless precision that rumors began circulating among those working on this project that they believed they were being guided by an unseen hand. Feverishly, Israel solicited the services of her most renowned architects. After being assembled, they began drafting the complex plans necessary to construct the new elaborate temple. This project also appeared to be functioning under supernatural assistance. What had been expected to take over a year-and-a-half, while working round the clock, was completed in just a few months. More amazing than either the site work or the architectural renderings was the actual construction of the new temple. Engineers and highly skilled construction personnel all testified to the unusual absence of routine problems that are associated with projects of this magnitude. Tasks that normally took days were being completed in hours. Things were progressing at such a rapid pace that some began to question the rumors of divine intervention and were instead becoming suspicious that perhaps the zeal to have a new temple was causing those in charge to cut corners in order to save time.

To quell the spread of those rumors a team of independent engineers from outside Israel was brought in to analyze every phase of the work in progress. They too were astonished at what they saw taking place. After carefully inspecting all the processes employed by the Jewish engineers and craftsmen, they concluded this was the most *remarkable engineering feat they had ever witnessed. They too used language that testified to the strange sense of a supernatural presence that seemed almost tangible whenever you stepped foot on the ancient site. The word "eerie" seemed to be a popular remark that many used when describing this unusual force.*

Excitement began mounting as the final phase of construction was drawing to a close. There was an international buzz that began circulating about this new temple. As momentum continued to increase, the new world leader seemed to take unusual interest in this project. His frequent visits and gracious remarks were well-received by government officials and brought much encouragement to its people. They were taken by surprise when The Leader went on a major international public television network and strongly encouraged all Jews living abroad to return to their ancestral homeland. He offered financial assistance, guaranteed jobs and even promised special housing for those willing to return. This all seemed too good to be true. The Israeli immigration office was overwhelmed with the response from his appeal and had to work overtime to process all the requests for new citizenship. Even the mass immigration of the early nineties paled in comparison to this new wave of Jewish immigrants.

Peace and prosperity began flourishing all over Israel (Ez.38:8b). Because of the special attention it was receiving from The Leader, Israel's popularity and influence abroad began to increase (Ez.38:12). Record trade agreements were being negotiated and as a result Israel's people began to sense a surge of optimism unprecedented in their brief history as a re-formed nation. The special attention The Leader was lavishing upon her was both flattering and intoxicating.

117

In the midst of this fresh swirl of budding popularity and success, arose the dissenting voice of the Messianic Jewish minority. Their growing offense at what was happening began prompting them to be more aggressive in their attempts to be heard. This was highly irritating and was becoming more and more offensive to their fellow Jewish brethren. The Messianic Believers had always been a thorn in the side of the Jewish community and their warnings were deeply resented by the nation at large. Their message of a crucified Messiah was appalling and public opinion was growing that drastic measures were needed to silence this band of discontents. High level governmental meetings began to take place about how this matter should be handled. Legislation was drafted that would impose both fines and stiff prison sentences upon those who continued to engage in public speech about this Messiah. There was unified agreement that strong action was required to silence, once and for all, these unruly dissenters.

The Messianic Jews' appeal for the people of Israel to turn from their sins and receive their crucified Messiah was unimaginably insulting to most Jews. They took great pride in their religious traditions and no rag-tag group of spiritual zealots was going to persuade them otherwise. Besides, their new temple was getting ready to be dedicated any day now and they had important matters on which to devote their attention.

Finally, the day all Israel longed for arrived. News teams from all over the world began arriving to broadcast this historic event. Dignitaries from nearly every nation responded to Israel's invitation. Israel was promoting this as the ushering in of a new age.

In order to reenact the dedication of Solomon's Temple (2 Chron. 7) there were special religious ceremonies that were scheduled to last seven days. This was to be followed by a day of solemn assembly which would be followed by an elaborate seven day celebration. Israel had spared no expense in promoting this dedication. The host of governmental and religious attendees from around the world along with the impressive list of international celebrities was staggering. All noted that nothing quite like this gathering had ever taken place and perhaps was even unique in world history. They were also aware that none of this would have been possible were it not for the attention given by The Leader (Isa.28:15). His skill at resolving delicate matters was nothing less than brilliant.

 For years the Jewish people had been preparing for this moment. Most of the early pioneers were now considered fringe and extremist. Every year these spiritual zealots had drawn national attention by attempting to lay the cornerstone for their new temple. These efforts were always met with swift resistance from Jewish authorities. This was during the years of considerable trouble and escalating hostilities with their Arab neighbors. Things were quite tense back in those days.

 Now, however, there is a totally new atmosphere of peace and safety, even with surrounding Arab neighbors (1 Thess.5:3). This could not have happened without the assistance of this charismatic new leader. His personal involvement and hands-on leadership over the temple's construction proved very helpful.

 Then, one of the oddest and most unexpected things took place. During the middle of one of the dedication ceremonies a single assassin lunged at The Leader with a small sword in his hand. The sword found its mark and sunk deep into the leader's head. His death appeared to be instantaneous (Rev.13:3). The whole scene was caught on tape and shown continuously on prime time news channels across the world. The entire international community was in a state of shock. Just as quickly as he had come on the scene, he was violently removed.

The following day his spiritual advisor (the false prophet) and traveling companion called together the media and when they arrived they found the slain leader lying on a colorfully decorated bed. No one could have prepared himself for what happened next. With the cameras rolling and hundreds of witnesses in attendance, his spiritual advisor leaned over and whispered something in his ear. For a moment there was a brief pause, and then slowly The Leader sat up, swung his legs off the bed and stood to his feet. The room went completely silent. A sense of awe was experienced by everyone in the room. The Advisor quickly spoke up and told everyone to return that evening and they would witness something even more powerful. With those brief remarks, both The Leader and his Advisor quickly exited the room leaving behind a crowd of stunned onlookers.

When they returned that evening, security people were everywhere and in the middle of the room stood a life-size statue of the slain leader. The Advisor had requested this and all were amazed at how quickly the task had been completed. Beside the statue stood a lectern and two elaborate chairs were strategically placed behind the podium. These had also been arranged by The Advisor and were placed exactly where he had instructed. When the security force had everyone seated and the room was secure, both The Leader and his Advisor quickly made their way from a side entrance and took their seats. Because there had been no explanation of what had occurred earlier, everyone was a bit disoriented and could only speculate what was going to take place that evening. The only information people had received led them to believe that whatever was getting ready to take place would be spectacular. They would not be disappointed.

The Leader remained seated beside the statue while his Advisor made his way to the podium. All could see the fresh wound on The Leader's head and marveled that it didn't seem to bother him. The Advisor cleared his throat and was extremely brief. What he actually said few could remember, however, what he did during the next few minutes, few could forget. He began by reminding the people of what had transpired that morning and he underscored the miracle they had witnessed and even caught on tape. He told them that only God could have done such an amazing work and if they watched closely they would see even greater things.

No sooner had he uttered those words than the statue, clearly made out of some kind of ceramic material, began speaking and proclaiming that The Leader was God. The fact that they were hearing this from a talking, lifeless statue validated this claim beyond all doubt (Rev.13:15).

You could hear the entire room fill with gasps as shock waves gripped everyone simultaneously. No one could believe what he was seeing. Getting a grip on their emotions was quite a challenge. Their minds were saying that this is nothing more than an elaborate hoax; however, their eyes were watching a talking ceramic statue. There was a total disconnect between what they were seeing and what they knew to be true. They all sat momentarily transfixed as if in a state of suspended animation. Everything that was taking place was happening in real time and was being broadcast live on satellite television. Therefore, what was happening in the room was happening, *simultaneously, in homes all across the world. As soon as reporters were able to gather their wits about them, they frantically began scribbling notes.*

The evening ended with The Advisor inviting everyone to join him at the new Jewish temple the following morning. With that brief announcement both The Leader and his Advisor made their way through a mob of security personnel and disappeared. Talk about "shock and awe." The room could not have been more bewildered and disoriented if little green men from the planet Zorb had landed. This was surreal. The conversations that started up sounded more like sanity checks then anything else. The room was experiencing a corporate, "What was that?" People were curious to see what the other person saw before they were willing to divulge what it was that they thought they might have possibly seen.

The next day, the Temple Mount area was standing room only as far as the eye could see. The Ben Gurion airport in Tel Aviv was booked solid with people who had watched the happenings of the previous day and felt they needed to be in Jerusalem to witness things first hand. The entire city was in a state of shock. The most confused of all were the Jewish people. After all, this was transpiring while they were attempting to complete their temple dedication. They too had to process the events of the past twenty-four hours and not much was making any sense at the moment.

Because of the immense crowd that started gathering before sunrise, television crews were forced to stay up all night to secure prime locations and to protect their equipment. The energy in the air was electrifying. You could clearly pick out a full-range of emotions at work in those who had gathered. Excitement, fear, joy, disillusionment, perplexity, anticipation; all these and more were in abundant supply. Occasionally you would lock eyes with one of the Jewish rabbis who was present, and you could detect an unusual air of discomfort. It was as if he intuitively knew something sinister was getting ready to happen.

The stage that had been constructed to host speakers for the temple dedication slowly began filling with a new set of faces. The two most recognizable were The Leader and his Advisor. Once again it was The Advisor who spoke first. His speech sounded much like the night before. He kept alluding to the deity of the leader and the international community needing to receive him as God. Then he startled everyone when he said that he was aware that many were still skeptical and needed further proof that The Leader was truly God. Before he took another breath he shouted, "F-i-r-e!" and immediately something similar to a bolt of lightening came from heaven, however, unlike lightening, whatever it was lasted over thirty seconds. The sound was deafening and the visual was unlike any lightening bolt ever seen by human eyes (Rev.13:13). To make things even more convincing, there wasn't a cloud in the sky. Everyone knew they had seen a genuine sign from heaven.

Then he turned around and calmly walked back to his seat. As soon as he was seated The Leader made his way up to the lectern and simply stared at everyone for a moment before he started talking. It wasn't like he was trying to gather his thoughts; it was really quite an odd look and very hard to explain with words. It was as if he communicated volumes without even saying a single word. His very presence carried such an air of confidence and reassurance that he was exceptionally disarming. The crowd sat mesmerized as if they had been lulled into some sort of hypnotic trance.

He told the crowd that the world had now entered into an entirely new era. He said that this new age would be a time of unprecedented peace, safety and prosperity (1Thess.5:3). He also said that the world had been desperately wanting and needing peace and everyone who had tried to create it had failed. He mentioned that Mohammad had tried and failed. That Abraham and Moses had tried and failed. That Jesus Christ had tried and failed. That all the Popes who had ever lived had tried and failed. That many cults and false spiritual leaders had tried and failed. That the only one who could ever bring true and lasting peace was God, and to do that, He would have to come to earth and live among them. After making that statement, he paused. At that moment the most eerie hush settled over the crowd. It seemed like there was an invisible presence hovering over the gathering. After he paused and slowly scanned the enormous crowd that had gathered, very calmly but with an uncanny boldness, he said, "Behold your God." As he said those words, his Advisor stood to his feet and shouted again, "F-i-r-e!" And again, the moment he shouted, fire came down from heaven and the roar of it was deafening (Rev.13:13). Just like the first bolt it lasted over thirty seconds. Then the strangest thing followed. The entire crowd heard a voice from heaven say, "The Leader is God ... listen to him" (Rev.13:14). In fact, the voice was so loud and clear that it was picked up by the television sound crews and was instantly broadcast around the entire world.

At that moment, The Advisor moved quickly to the podium, pointed to The Leader and repeated over and over, "Behold your God," ... "Behold your God" ... "Behold your God" ... "Behold your God."

The entire crowd picked up on this and joined in the chant and repeated this over and over for the next five to ten minutes. For a moment you felt like you were attending a rock concert rather than hearing a political speech. While they were chanting, The Leader stood smiling with approval and kept scanning the crowd with his eyes.

The crowd was so mesmerized by its chanting that hardly anyone seemed to notice that a perfect rainbow had formed (Rev.13:14) and spanned from one end of the crowd to the other with the temple positioned right in the center. When the crowd finally became aware, the volume grew louder and louder. People were all silently thinking, "Who could do something this perfect but God Himself?"

No one could have predicted what would happen next. The Leader turned and walked right into the new temple. Television crews with mobile cameras followed. Although he disappeared inside he was clearly visible on the huge screens that were positioned beside the stage. It was obvious that he knew exactly where he was going; he was heading straight for the Holy of Holies. You could hear the gasps of the rabbis who were present. The thought of a Gentile daring to walk into a holy Jewish temple caught them completely off guard. The Leader stopped momentarily as he entered the Holy Place, slowly scanning the room, as if making sure everything was present and nothing missing or out of order. He then paused again as he reached the veil. The only thing now separating The Leader from entering the Jews' most holy area was a few inches of elaborately decorated tapestry.

Outside, the crowd was motionless and nearly breathless. The Jews were well aware that if anyone but their appointed High Priest attempted to enter the Holy of Holies, that individual would be struck dead immediately; that is, unless he were God.

The Leader gave a quick hand motion and several of his security guards appeared. They took hold of the veil and violently tore it from its ceiling attachments and then it was quickly removed. Other guards appeared carrying what could only be described as a portable throne. The Leader took his seat (2 Thess.2:4) and faced the cameras.

Outside, religious Jews began to weep, secular Jews seemed puzzled and disoriented, and the rest appeared to be totally caught up in the drama, living each moment as it unfolded. Although those in attendance ran the entire spectrum emotionally, the one thing that seemed common in this diverse crowd was the understanding that they were watching history in the making.

The Leader began speaking about how peace and safety (1 Thess. 5:3) would be the highest priority under his administration. He let them know that although they had been experiencing a measure of peace that much more needed to be done in order to secure true and lasting peace. To do so, he said, would require bold new policies and sweeping reforms in order to guarantee and maintain peace and safety for every citizen on the earth.

He then abruptly switched tracks and began mocking other religious groups and labeled them all as counterfeits and pretenders. He said the proof of their deceit was that their religious creeds had always produced wars and strife. These are the greatest obstacles to peace and safety, he said. Then he became even more direct when mentioning two groups in particular. He held them ultimately responsible for stirring up hatred and being full of intolerance. These, he said, had been the biggest contributors to global unrest and instability. Because Christianity and Judaism follow a book of lies (2 Thess.2:10) they are responsible for more injustices and for *causing more wars than any other group in the history of mankind, he declared. He went on to say that for the sake of peace he would outlaw all false religions and deal ruthlessly with any who try to go back to the old order and continue to serve false gods. "This is a new day," he said. "This is my temple and without me this temple could never have been built."*

Outside the people were silent and were thinking to themselves what all this meant. They were wondering what these sweeping reforms might look like and how they might affect their individual lives. This produced a moment of unrest. Sensing what was happening, The Advisor returned to the podium and began to again proclaim what an honor it was for the nations to be alive at a time when God himself was willing to come and live among them. Who else could die and be raised back to life (Rev.13:12) but God? "Worship The Leader," he said. "He alone is God. Serve him or receive his wrath." With those words, the ground began to tremble and again for a third time, a huge flame of fire shot from heaven and the sound again was deafening. Somewhere in the crowd a chant started. Although it started off quietly, it soon grew and became a thunderous roar, "The Leader - he is God – we will serve none other." Over and over they repeated this chant. The longer it continued, the stronger and louder it became.

Author's Note:
The event the Bible calls the *"abomination of desolation"* (Dan.11:31) is the turning point that ushers in the Great Tribulation. The *"abomination"* part takes place with the defilement of the newly built Jewish temple. Scripture is silent as to how long the temple will be in operation before this event actually takes place. It obviously can't be

operating very long because there is a three-and-a-half year timeline in which major changes take place. First, a pseudo-peace must be established (Ez.38:8b, 1 Thess.5:3). Secondly, I can only surmise that an amazing covenant must be negotiated that calls for the removal of all Muslim holy shrines from the Temple Mount area and which authorizes Israel to build a third temple (The Tribulation Temple). Thirdly, the Muslim holy shrines must be dismantled and removed (they will certainly be dismantled and not demolished as some have speculated). Fourth, the Jews must draft plans, work exhaustively to prepare the site and then construct their temple. Finally, the temple must be in full use for some unspecified period of time before the Antichrist seizes control for his own purposes (2 Thess.2:3-5). As you can see, for all this to be accomplished in a three-and-a-half-year time span, things must develop quickly. In fact, I believe the only way this could happen is with supernatural assistance. Because Satan knows he is working on a tight time schedule (Rev.12:12), instead of resistance he will actually offer demonic assistance to ensure things progress at an unusually fast pace. After the Antichrist desecrates the newly built Jewish Tribulation Temple, the earth will prepare to experience the most violent season it has ever known (Dan.12:1; Matt.24:21-22).

CHAPTER 10

Book of Revelation Overview

"Opinions about the Book of Revelation cover a huge spectrum. When put together, it seems impossible that they all refer to the same piece of literature." [2]

"We boldly affirm that the study of this book would present absolutely no possibility of error if the inconceivable, often ridiculous, prejudice of theologians in all ages had not so trammeled it and made it bristle with difficulties that most readers shrink from it in alarm. Apart from these preconceptions, the Revelation would be the most simple, most transparent book that prophet ever penned." [3]

"It is one of the great misfortunes of our expertise-oriented culture that when anything seems difficult it is sent off to the university to be figured out." [4]

No single book in the Bible has ever been more misunderstood and thus neglected than the Book of Revelation. Rather than being tried and found wanting, this book has been woefully neglected and thus its treasures have remained in tact and untouched. The Book of Revelation was never written for college professors, it was

[2] David Pawson, Pg 85 *When Jesus Returns* – Hodder & Stoughton Ltd, published 1995

[3] Reuss (1884), quoted in *The Prophecy Handbook* – World Bible Publishers 1991

[4] Eugene Paterson, Pg 200 *Reversed Thunder* – Harper Collins, published 1988

written and intended to be understood by the ordinary Believer (1 Cor.1:26). I have spent literally hundreds of hours wading through commentaries that seem to have been written by brilliant men whose primary preoccupation in life appears to be how to take simple truth and see how complex and confusing they can make it. Not much has changed since biblical times. The common people still hear Him gladly (Mk.12:37).

One of my primary goals throughout this book has been to make end time subjects as clear and understandable as possible. I will let the reader decide the degree of success I have had in achieving that objective. Understanding the Book of Revelation has little to do with I.Q. and academic achievements. This book yields its greatest treasures to those who approach it in simple faith, with a humble heart and a tender spirit.

Many are discouraged by the few difficult passages in the book and walk away leaving the vast majority of the book still sitting on the table completely untouched. Jesus called that *"Straining at gnats and swallowing camels"* (Matt.23:24). I would encourage you to gain as much understanding as possible and refuse to get thrown off course or discouraged by the few verses that you find challenging. My personal belief is that there are portions of end time prophetic scripture that are intentionally hidden by God and will be released on a need-to-know basis. There was information that God forbade Daniel from recording and he was told that some things would remain secret until the last days (Dan.8:26; 9:24; 12:4, 9). We don't need to concern ourselves as to when this additional information will be released. Rather, we would be wise to gain as much understanding as God will permit now so that the added insights will have an adequate foundation on which to stand.

> *Daniel answered and said: "Blessed be the name of God forever and ever, for wisdom and might are His. (21) And He changes the times and the seasons; He removes kings and raises up kings; He gives wisdom to the wise And knowledge to those who have understanding. (22) He reveals deep and secret things; He knows what is in the darkness, and light dwells with Him (Dan.2:20-22)*

Please note who God lavishes revelation upon. We generally assume that He would give wisdom to those who lack it and supply knowledge to the unknowledgeable. The biblical pattern, however, is that God loves to increase and add to the understanding we have already obtained by diligently seeking His heart (Mk.4:24). God delights to reward the hungry seeker (Heb.11:6). Nowhere is this more evident than when it comes to those who refuse to be denied access to the hidden manna of the Book of Revelation. Prepare your heart for a lifetime of discovery and fascination.

Although this book was clearly written for Believers of every generation, it is intended to be exceptionally helpful for those living in the generation in which the Lord returns. The Book of Revelation is constructed in such a way that it functions as an end time training manual and is specifically designed to equip the last generation for martyrdom (Rev.13:7). Many more saints will lay down their lives, in the will of God, than will survive the Great

Tribulation (Dan. 7:21,25). Consequently, one of the key features of this book is the call for patient endurance among the saints of God (Rev.14:12). The letters to the seven churches in chapters two and three offer strong incentives to those who overcome and persevere through great hardship. Although the exhortations were historically directed to seven actual churches in Asia Minor, (Turkey today), the message was clearly intended to be an encouragement to all saints experiencing severe persecution.

Let's Get Started

One of the most helpful things that you must understand about the Book of Revelation is how the book is laid out. Jumping into this book without some basic information would be like jumping into the deep end of an Olympic size swimming pool before knowing how to swim. Your zeal will diminish rapidly as you struggle to keep your head above water. With just a few simple instructions you will have the time of your life.

The book's outline looks like this:

1. Introduction (Rev. 1)
2. Letters to churches (Rev. 2-3)
3. The heavenly court (Rev. 4-5)
4. Great Tribulation (Rev. 6-19)
5. The Second Coming (Rev. 19:11-21)
6. The Millennial Kingdom and White Throne Judgment (Rev. 20)
7. The New Jerusalem (Rev. 21-22)

The book's structure looks like this:
There are 5 chronological sections:
a. Rev. 6:1-17
b. Rev. 8:1- 9:21
c. Rev. 11:15-19
d. Rev. 16:1-21
e. Rev. 19:11-21:8

Chronological Section Notes:
- I have discovered that marking or highlighting these in my Bible is helpful
- The events in these sections unfold chronologically and sequentially
- The basic truths in these sections are not difficult to understand
- The 21 numbered judgments unfold sequentially (1-2-3 etc.)
- These are given in a straightforward way for the purpose of clarity

There are 5 parenthetical sections:
a. Rev. 7:1-17
b. Rev. 10:1 - 11:13
c. Rev. 12:1- 14:20
d. Rev. 17:1- 19:10
e. Rev. 21:9 – 22:5

Parenthetical Section Notes:
The parenthetical sections are generally the most difficult to understand
These are provided for the purpose of instruction and are intended to answer two basic questions:
- Why are God's judgments so severe?

• What will happen to the church?

The different sections answer these questions in creative ways and are pastoral in purpose. Think of these like pressing the "pause button" on a remote control. The angel sees that John is struggling with information overload and so he stops and takes time to explain these troubling events to John. When John is able to gather himself emotionally, the angel hits "play" and the story line picks back up again.

Twenty-One Numbered Judgments
(listed in three categories)

Three Numbered Judgments
(Seals, Trumpets and Bowls)

Seals
White horse – Antichrist's political / military power
Red horse – Wars & global bloodshed
Black horse – Famine & economic crisis
Pale horse – Disease & death for 1/4 earth
Prayer movement – Releasing judgments (intercession)
Cosmic disturbances – Cosmic crisis
Heaven silenced – Prayers of saints listened to

Trumpets
1/3 vegetation burned up
1/3 seas destroyed
1/3 earth's fresh water poisoned
1/3 earth's light darkened
Demonic plague of locusts released
1/3 earth's population slain
Church removed - given resurrected bodies

[Second Coming Procession begins]
Bowls
Sores on Antichrist worshippers
Seas turn to blood - all sea life dies
Fresh water turns to blood
Scorching heat
Darkness covers Antichrist's empire
Demons lure nations to Armageddon
Global earthquake - hail stones

Notes on these twenty-one numbered judgments:

- They will unfold chronologically
(Seals first, trumpets follow seals, bowls follow trumpets)
- Each of the judgment series has seven distinct actions
- They will unfold sequentially
The first seal will be followed by seals 2, 3, 4, 5, 6, 7; trumpet one will come immediately before trumpets 2, 3, 4, 5, 6, 7; the first bowl will precede bowls 2, 3, 4, 5, 6, 7
- The judgments seem to increase in both intensity and scope

Seven Primary Symbols of the Book of Revelation

Note: All the events and numbers in Revelation are intended to be taken and understood in their plain meaning (literal sense) *unless specifically indicated to be interpreted symbolically* (i.e. Rev. 1:20; 5:6; 11:8; 12:1, 3, 9; 17:7, 9). To help simplify, Daniel used many of the same symbols and if you cross reference these you will find it helps bring clarity to the meanings in Revelation. The Bible is brilliant in the way it serves to interpret itself. Bible commentators who use the literal interpretation method have general agreement over the use of its symbols. Interpreters who take the approach that the Book of Revelation is to be taken symbolically rather than literally, vary greatly in their use and understanding of their symbols and therefore seem to engage in academic debates among themselves, attempting to defend their highly subjective conclusions. I recommend the literal view as it is much less cumbersome and will take you much deeper, much faster.

1. **The Dragon**: is always symbolic of *Satan* (Rev. 12:3, 4, 7, 9, 13, 16, 17; 13:2; 16:13; 20:2)

2. **The First Beast:** is symbolic of the *Antichrist*. He is called the Beast 36 times in the Book of Revelation (Rev. 13; 14:9-11; 17:3-17; 19:19-21; 20:4, 10)

3. **Another Beast**: is symbolic of the individual known as the *False Prophet* and is only referred to as Another Beast once. Every other mention of him in scripture refers to him as the *False Prophet* (Rev. 13;11-17;16:13; 19:20; 20:10)

4. **The 7 heads**: are symbolic of the seven world empires who historically have been great enemies of Israel. Most Bible teachers identify these as (1) Egypt (2) Assyria (3) Babylon (4) Persia (5) Greece (6) Rome (7) Revived Roman Empire (Dan. 2:41-42; 7:7, 20, 24; Rev. 12:3; 13:1; 17:3-16)

5. **The 10 horns**: are symbolic of a 10 nation confederation which will be under the control and totally submitted to the Antichrist's authority. Exactly which nations they are is

unclear. Much speculation has centered around identifying them. (Dan. 2:41-42; 7:7; 11:20, 24, 36-45; Rev. 12:3; 13:1; 17:3, 7, 12, 16)

6. **The Harlot Babylon**: is the literal city of Babylon located today in Iraq and situated on the Euphrates River (50 miles south of Baghdad). It will be one of the most wicked cities on earth. It will become an economic power-house and will be the future home of one of the Antichrist's headquarters. Babylon will be destroyed in one day by divine judgment (Rev. 17-18; Isa.13-14; 21; Jer.50-51)

7. **The Woman with the Male-child**: the woman is the faithful remnant of Israel throughout history (Rev. 12:1-5; 19:7-8). The Male Child is Jesus (Rev.12:4-5). The rest of her offspring with whom Satan makes war are Gentile Believers during the Great Tribulation (Rev.12:17)

If someone had shared the information I just shared with you when I was a new Believer, my studies of the Book of Revelation would have gone to unimaginable heights and been an absolute joy. Trying to decipher the truth from many of today's authors about this book has been one of the most frustrating journeys of my Christian experience.

You, on the other hand, are now armed and dangerous. If you simply separate the parenthetical sections from the chronological sections, use a common sense approach and understand the seven symbols that I just shared with you, then you are ready to make some serious progress.

Please always keep in the forefront that the Book of Revelation is about the revelation of a person. It has one hero and His glory is sown throughout the pages of the entire book, chapter by chapter, verse by verse and line by line. If you ever lose sight of that, you run the risk of becoming a contemporary Pharisee. Paul described them as, *"always learning and never able to come to the knowledge of the truth" (2 Tim.3:7).* The Book of Revelation is the revelation of Jesus Christ and Him alone. He is the only one able, worthy and trusted by the Father to take the scroll of mankind's redemptive history (Rev.5:7) and bring it to its full and glorious conclusion. When you get an ounce of revelation about your future in God's marvelous plan, it will make every cell in your body sing out:

> *You are worthy to take the scroll, and to open its seals; for You were slain, and have redeemed us to God by Your blood out of every tribe and tongue and people and nation, (10) And have made us kings and priests to our God; And we shall reign on the earth*
> *(Rev. 5:9-10)*

Birth Pangs | Tribulation Period | Age Transition

Intensification
Global Calamities

1st 3 1/2 Years
Rise of Antichrist
Rise of False Prophet
Covenant of Death
Temple Built
Fatal Head Wound
Antichrist Resurrected
Talking Statue
Mark of the Beast

2nd 3 1/2 Years
Abomination of Desolation
Two Witnesses
Twenty One Numbered Judgments
Intense Persecution
Church Raptured at Seventh Trumpet

Judgment Seat of Christ
Marriage Supper
Second Coming
Procession
Enemies Destroyed
Satan Bound
Antichrist Lake of Fire
False Prophet Lake of Fire
Jewish People Judged
Saints - Glorified Bodies
Jewish Salvation
Earth's Topography Changed

Millennial Kingdom → Age Transition → New Jerusalem

Millennial Kingdom

1,000 Year Reign
Saints Rule and Reign
Animal Kingdom Reformation
Life Cycle Radically Increased
Ecological Systems Altered
People in Natural Bodies
People in Resurrected Bodies
Jerusalem Millennial Capital City
Garden of Eden
Feasts Celebrated
Temple Worship Restored
Jesus Millennial Seminars
Sin Minimized

Age Transition

Satan Paroled
Global Rebellion
Jesus Subdues Rebellion
Last Enemy Defeated (Death)
Satan - Lake of Fire
Great White Throne Judgment
* Unbelievers
* Millennial Saints (?)
Millennial Saints Glorified (?)
Old Earth Burned Up
Old Heavens Destroyed

New Jerusalem

New Heavens
New Earth
New Jerusalem Comes to Earth
No Sun or Moon
Jesus Glory Lights Up New Jerusalem
Saints Rule and Reign Forever
All Sin Removed

CHAPTER 11

The Great Tribulation

*"I have been in countries where the saints
are already suffering terrible persecution. In
China the Christians were told, 'Don't
worry, before the Tribulation comes you will
be translated, raptured.' Then came terrible
persecution. Millions of Christians were
tortured to death. Later I heard a Bishop
from China say, sadly: 'We have failed. We
should have made the people strong for
persecution rather than telling them that
Jesus would come first.' Turning to me, he
said: 'Tell the people how to be strong in
times of persecution, how to stand when the
Tribulation comes – to stand and not faint.' I
feel that I have a divine mandate to go and
tell the people of this world that it is possible
to be strong in the Lord Jesus Christ. We are
in training for the Tribulation. Since I have
gone already through prison for Jesus' sake,
and since I met that Bishop from China, now
every time I read a good Bible text I think:
'Hey, I can use that in the time of
Tribulation.' Then I write it down and learn
it by heart."* [5]

---

[5] Corrie Ten Boom, Pg 199 *When Jesus Returns*

> *For then there will be great tribulation, such as has not been since the beginning of the world until this time, no, nor ever shall be. (22) And unless those days were shortened, no flesh would be saved; but for the elect's sake those days will be shortened (Matt.24:21-22)*

The Tribulation Period is a time that will be unpacked in two installments. The length of the entire period is seven years (Dan.9:24-26). This time line will be played out in two equal sections of time. Both of these sections will last three-and-a- half years. Sometimes the term *"time, times, and a half time"* is used, and other scriptures use the notation *"one thousand two hundred and sixty days."* Either way it is presented, it is seven years in duration. The first three-and-a-half year period is a time when the Antichrist will be busy establishing his political, economic, religious and military power base. This will be the proverbial calm before the storm. What is going on will mostly be covert. Although there will be a flurry of activity happening behind the scenes in the form of political posturing and secret alliances being set in place, little will be noticeable to the casual observer.

The turning point will come immediately following Israel's new temple dedication. The Antichrist will seize control of the temple and commit a heinous act which the Bible calls the Abomination of Desolation (Dan.12:11).

Exactly What Is The Abomination Jesus Warned About?

For years, I wrestled with what that despicable act might actually look like. I just assumed it was the enactment of 2 Thessalonians 2:4. This verse describes the Antichrist, after his hostile take over of the newly-completed Jewish Temple in Jerusalem, sitting in the Holy of Holies spewing slanderous denials about the true and living God, while promoting himself as the real God. My false assumption was that this act of blasphemy was considered to be the deed referred to as the Abomination of Desolation. Let me show you where I am going with this.

> *...then they shall take away the daily sacrifices, and **place there** the abomination of desolation*
> *(Dan.11:31)*

> *And from the time that the daily sacrifice is taken away, and the abomination of desolation **is set up***
> *(Dan.12:11)*

> *Therefore when you see the 'abomination of desolation,' ... **standing** in the holy place*
> *(Matt.24:15)*

Whatever form this abomination will take, it is clearly: (1) placed (2) set-up and (3) remains standing in the new temple. The only incident mentioned in scripture that seems related to this event is the bizarre scene that is described in Revelation 13:15. The more I meditate on this passage, the more I am convinced it has real merit.

> *He [the false prophet beast] was granted power to give breath to the image of the beast, that the image of the beast should both*

> *speak and cause as many as would not worship the image of the beast to be killed.*

We are not told what material this image will be made of, only that it will be an image (exact replica) of the new world leader (Rev.13:14). I have a hunch it will be a life-size image, perhaps larger than life, and will be either chiseled out of rock and have a rustic look or be ceramic and covered with gold. Whatever substance this image is made of, it will be on display for the entire world to view. Satan will be given authority to cause this image to demand, not just suggest or request, that all people give homage to the Political Beast or be killed (Rev.13:15).

Notice the evil chain of command, as well as the events that are being highlighted here. Satan inspires the False Prophet to have a statue crafted that is an exact likeness of the Political Leader. The reason for this image being constructed is to celebrate the Leader's miraculous recovery after surviving a lethal head wound suffered during an assassination attempt (Rev.13:1-15).

Check out the demonic cycle described here. Operating under satanic inspiration, the False Prophet makes an idol. The idol is then given satanic powers to speak and thus proclaim the deity of the Antichrist.

The Great Counterfeit

*The dragon [Satan] gave him [the Antichrist] his **power**, his **throne,** and great **authority***
(Rev.13:2)

Do you see what is happening? Satan is attempting to counterfeit the ministry of Jesus. His dark kingdom experienced massive disruption when Jesus released His power and authority on his people and they went out and did supernatural signs and wonders. Satan was taking notes and has decided that he is going to release an end time supernatural display of power through his unholy trinity consisting of himself, the Antichrist and the False Prophet. Satan, unlike God, doesn't have a creative bone in his wicked body. He can only copy.

Then He called His twelve disciples together and gave them power and authority over all demons, and to cure diseases
(Luke 9:1-2)

Behold, I give you the authority to trample on serpents and scorpions, and over all the power of the enemy, and nothing shall by any means hurt you
(Luke 10:19-20)

Satan's Most Valued Possession

The really interesting declaration contained in the Rev.13:2 verse is about something that most of us never noticed or understood before. Not only has the Devil promised to give the Antichrist a measure of satanic power and authority but he has promised to share with him his most treasured possession. "What would that be?" someone might ask. I have absolutely no doubt that the Antichrist entered into a secret pact with Satan. The same offer that the devil made to Jesus, he will certainly make again

(Matt.3:8-9). Although his offer was flatly rejected by Jesus, the Antichrist will jump at this new opportunity. The Devil's gifts never come cheap, and these will cost the Antichrist his very soul. In return, he will receive Satan's most-valued possession. He will be given exclusive rights to sit on Satan's throne.

Remember, Satan's primary ambition and driving motivation have never changed. He has always wanted full control of God's creation. Also remember, he has absolutely no creative abilities whatsoever. Therefore, he can only gain legal access through sin. Wherever sin is present, he is granted spiritual access. Wherever sin is absent, he has no jurisdiction (Jn.14:30). This is why he has no possibility of success in God's heavenly realm.

> *How you are fallen from heaven, O Lucifer, [Satan] son of the morning! How you are cut down to the ground [cast out of God's presence], you who weakened the nations! (13) For you have said in your heart: **I will** ascend into heaven, **I will** exalt my throne above the stars of God; **I will** also sit on the mount of the congregation on the farthest sides of the north; (14) **I will** ascend above the heights of the clouds, **I will** be like the Most High*
> *(Isa.14:12-14)*

My next statement will be much better understood after you have examined the section on the coming Millennial Kingdom. When you compare these verses in Isaiah with those of Psalm 48, as well as other millennial text, you will quickly discover what is happening. The most diabolical and ambitious plan ever devised in Satan's heart is his obsession to rule, as God, while sitting on God's throne. Thrones have always been a sign of power and authority. Thrones denote who has ultimate and complete control.

Satan's Counterfeit Throne

Our adversary is very aware of Jesus' intention to return to earth and rule the earth from His throne in Jerusalem (Matt.19:28). I will validate this next statement later, but guess where the exact location of Jesus' throne will be? It will be located in Jerusalem, on the thirty-three acres called the Temple Mount, in the newly constructed Millennial Temple complex, and specifically in the chamber known as the Holy of Holies. Guess where Satan intends to set up his throne from which to rule the entire earth? You guessed it, the exact same location. Like I mentioned earlier, Satan has never had a creative thought in his entire existence.

Satan's elaborate end time plan has two key elements. The first involves hijacking the most sacred square footage of real estate on the planet for the purpose of setting up his throne on earth. He is well aware that the Temple Mount area in Jerusalem is the most contested spiritual power base on earth and he fully intends to subdue and control that area. Secondly, after seizing control through his puppet leader, the Antichrist, his next order of business is the full and total elimination of every single Jewish person. This is his primary strategy as it enables him to maintain his position of world domination. The Antichrist will be like Adolf Hitler on steroids when it comes to his unabashed hatred for the Jews. If this plan

147

fails he fully understands the consequences. Since we covered this subject extensively in chapter eight, we will abandon this for now. You will understand the bigger picture later.

Back to the Abomination of Desolation

We still have some unfinished business with the statue sitting in the temple. Guess where the Antichrist and the False Prophet decide to place this wicked abomination?

> *Therefore when you see the 'abomination of desolation,' ...* ***standing in the holy place*** *(Matt.24:15)*

It appears that the Antichrist will set up shop in the Holy of Holies and will put the talking image, the abomination of desolation, next door in the Holy Place. In order to do that he will need to remove the furniture that God's Word commands to occupy that sacred chamber. The Altar of Incense, the Table of Showbread and the Golden Lamp Stand (Ex. 25) will all be removed in order to make room for the new life-sized idol.

The Earth's Darkest Days Begin

When all this begins to unfold, things on earth are preparing to go through the darkest period of time in history. Daniel prophesied that the last three-and-a-half years, or Great Tribulation, will go down as the most troubling time mankind has ever experienced (Dan.12:1). Jesus added that if God failed to intervene, the entire human race would be extinct. The Bible has several names for this dark hour. The most descriptive of these is found in the Book of the prophet Joel. He calls it, *"the great and very terrible day of the Lord"* (Joel 2:11).

God's Two-Fold Message

Just as you can find positive aspects associated with storms that produce massive patterns of destruction, the same will be true during the Great Tribulation. There is a reason Joel described this as *"The great and very terrible day of the Lord."* Mostly, this period of time receives a lot of negative press, and the good news gets buried on page ten, right beside the denture advertisement.

This will be the church's finest hour, as well as its most challenging. Jesus is after a purified Bride and this does not happen until Revelation 19:7. That means that there are a lot of things that must take place before Jesus receives the just reward of His suffering. If the Father were to present His precious Son with today's carnal, half-hearted, compromising, mostly backslidden and lukewarm Bride, what kind of statement would that make? Even human fathers want their sons to marry wholesome women who are passionately in love and deeply committed to their sons. Should God's standards be lower than ours? Think about it.

Why am I bringing this up? I have heard it said by many well-known Bible teachers that the church could be caught up at any moment and whisked away to glory. Could I insert straightforward questions here? My questions are extremely simple ones. Why would God want to do something like that? Is today's church the victorious church that His Son bled and died for? Doesn't the sacrificial death of Jesus on the cross deserve better? Do you think that

Jesus would mind putting up with a few hang-ups if His Father was willing to expedite the process a little? Sorry, but this reminds me of the same sinking feeling that I had when I left Vietnam. After going through the most difficult year of my life, I searched my soul and asked one probing question. Is Vietnam better off today than it was a year ago when I arrived? You know the answer.

The point is that God has a glorious solution for a church bound in compromise and riddled with sin. It's really not a new solution but it's the most effective. It's time tested and has an awesome success rate. Guess what it's called? It's called, "Big trouble!" Like my friend, Jamie Buckingham replied when asked by a reporter, "What is the surest sign of spiritual growth?" Jamie thought a moment, and then gave this simple yet wise one-word reply, "Pain." Anybody get a witness? I didn't think so.

Sorry for the lightheartedness, but I have a burning desire to see an empowered church, moving in signs and wonders and which is passionately in love with her Bridegroom King. The very thought of the Father offering today's defiled Bride for His Son's faithful sacrifice causes me deep inner pain. I am not attempting to be overly dramatic. I'm serious. Jesus deserves better and I am so encouraged by the Word of God because it assures me that He will indeed receive a Bride that is a fully-yoked companion and will serve Him with diligent devotion (Heb. 11:6).

Jesus Himself proclaimed, *"**This gospel** of the kingdom will be preached in all the world as a witness to all nations, and **THEN** the end will come"* (Matt.24:14). He was comparing similar qualities that identified His ministry to what will be happening at the end of the age just prior to His return. There are primarily two things that separate today's gospel presentation from that which Jesus proclaimed. They are, power and authority. When Jesus held a healing conference, the sick really got healed! There was a genuine demonstration of what was being taught. The words of the Apostle Paul should cut us to the heart.

> *And my speech and my preaching were not with persuasive words of human wisdom, but, (5) that your faith should not be in the wisdom of men but in the power of God*
> *(1 Cor.2:4-5)*

Beloved, how many of us, with integrity, could put this verse on our ministry brochures and not get sued for false advertising? Again, I'm really not trying to be cute or clever here. These are serious matters. A burden I carry is one that is difficult to discuss with most spiritual leaders today. The burden is called *"spiritual reality"* and it seems that many are extremely satisfied with shallow results as long as the offerings are up and the pews are full.

Where is the church that understood long hours of laboring in prayer? Where are the people who once believed that fasting and prayer are an essential part of the normal Christian life? Where are the people who stayed up late at night and rose early in the morning so they could meet with God? Where are the people who willingly sacrificed time, money and convenience in order to pursue wholehearted obedience? Church, these are not only valid questions but issues we must face squarely lest we leave the generation behind us a carnal legacy, unfit for Kingdom consumption.

Jesus mentioned a generation which would operate in unusual signs and wonders (Jn.14:12). The *"greater*

works" that He referred to were promised to a last day
church that is walking in a measure of godly humility so
that these works don't destroy them but are useful in
bringing many souls into the Kingdom (Ja.4:6). There will
be such a massive blitz of counterfeit miracles displayed
during the end times (2 Thess.2:9) that God will also be
releasing awesome displays of His power to counter the
demonic flood of lying signs and wonders. Just like *"the
magicians of Egypt"* (Ex. 7:11) were able to duplicate
many unusual signs, so it will be in the last days. Authentic
miracles and satanic signs and wonders will be happening
simultaneously. The Believers doing supernatural
manifestations will give all the glory to Jesus Christ.
Demonic lying-signs and wonders (2 Thess.2:9) will be
done in the name of the Antichrist and will be performed by
Satan himself (Rev.13:2).

So what's the point? The point is that the same
process God worked when He sent Elijah to confront the
false prophets at Mt. Carmel will be repeated with much
greater intensity in the last days.

> *Now therefore, send and gather all Israel to
> me on Mount Carmel ..., (20) so Ahab sent for
> all the children of Israel, and gathered the
> prophets together on Mount Carmel. (21) And
> Elijah came to all the people, and said,
> "How long will you falter between two
> opinions? If the LORD is God, follow Him;
> but if Baal, follow him"*
> *(1 Kings 18:19-21)*

The great issue facing those living at the end of the
age will be to whom are you going to pledge your life to

serve? There will only be two viable options. Those choosing to surrender their lives to Christ will do so with the full understanding that making that choice could lead to martyrdom. Those who yield to the pressure of the Antichrist will forfeit any possibility of salvation (Rev.14:11) and will be instantly possessed by a reprobate spirit. They will receive much more than they bargained for and will be loyal subjects of the prince of darkness. They will be sentenced at the Great White Throne Judgment, immediately following the Millennial Kingdom, to the Lake of Fire, commonly referred to as hell (Rev.20:11-15). It is a place of everlasting torment and is the ultimate destination of Satan and all his demonic forces (Rev.19:20). The residents of the Lake of Fire will be comprised of spirit beings as well as rebellious humans. Those who chose to live independent from God in this life will experience the terror of being separated from Him for eternity (Rev.20:15). There will be no second chances for those receiving the mark of the beast, *"As it is appointed for men to die once, but after this the judgment" (Heb.9:27).*

CHAPTER 12

The Great and Very Terrible Day of the Lord

The period of time that the Bible refers to as *"the Great Tribulation"* has many descriptive titles in scripture. Sometimes it is simply called, *"The day of the Lord"* (Jer.46:10). Other times it's called *"The time of Jacob's trouble"* (Jer.30:7). Although it is given many titles, none is more graphic than the one found in the Book of Joel. The prophet calls it *"The great and very terrible day of the Lord"* (Joel 2:11). He then adds a terrifying qualifier, *"Who can endure it?"*

The phrase, *"The day of the Lord,"* is a bit deceiving. Although there certainly is an actual day assigned for the great transition in which this current age will be concluded and the next begins, the normal usage of this phrase is specifically addressing a three-and-a-half year period of time. It begins with the *"abomination of desolation"* (Matt.24:15) and isn't completed until Jesus returns and subdues the entire earth (Ps.2). This will be the ultimate *"day of the Lord."*

This season of time will be both *"great and very terrible"* depending in whom you are placing your trust and confidence. It will be *"great"* for those who are fully devoted to Christ and *"very terrible"* for those who have yielded control of their lives to the Antichrist.

I want to do a quick fly over and briefly survey some of the events that the Bible predicts will be happening during this time. I intend to be concise and will keep my comments to a minimum. I encourage the reader to do more in-depth study on your own (Acts 17:11).

144,000 Jewish Apostolic Witnesses

Do not harm the earth, the sea, or the trees till we have sealed the servants of our God on their foreheads. (4) And I heard the number of those who were sealed. One hundred and forty-four thousand of all the tribes of the children of Israel were sealed (Rev.7:3-4)

Then I looked, and behold, a Lamb standing on Mount Zion, and with Him one hundred and forty-four thousand, having His Father's name written on their foreheads (Rev.14:1)

They sang as it were a new song before the throne, before the four living creatures, and the elders; and no one could learn that song except the hundred and forty-four thousand who were redeemed from the earth. (4) These are the ones who were not defiled with women, for they are virgins. These are the ones who follow the Lamb wherever He goes. These were redeemed from among men, being firstfruits to God and to the Lamb. (5) And in their mouth was found no deceit, for they are without fault before the throne of God (Rev.14:3-5)

Then I saw another angel flying in the midst
of heaven, having the everlasting gospel to
preach to those who dwell on the earth -- to
every nation, tribe, tongue, and people – (7)
saying with a loud voice, "Fear God and
give glory to Him, for the hour of His
judgment has come
(Rev.14:6-7)

Although this is one of the clearest accounts that is given in the Book of Revelation, it is incredible what many Bible scholars have tried to do to this portion of scripture. The most difficult part of this account is the re-introduction of the twelve tribes of Israel. These tribes have never been misplaced, replaced or off God's radar screen. He knows exactly who they are and He fully intends to restore the tribes supernaturally before the end of the age. Exactly how He plans to identify these tribes, we are not told and so we must wait and see. The tribes of Israel are totally Jewish, and despite the attempts of some misguided Gentiles to claim biblical rights of inclusion, these tribes will remain Jewish. The tribes will also have an active role to play in the Millennial Kingdom (Ez.40-48).

For everything we are not told about this extremely unique group, we do know some stunning information. There will be 12,000 taken from each of the twelve tribes. They are called *"the servants of God"* (Rev.7:3) and have the Father's name written on their foreheads (Rev.14:2). Because of this we know they will be a fiery group of Messianic Believers who have a strong relationship with God.

Because of their unique level of dedication they are allowed to learn a special worship song that no one else knows or is allowed to sing. We are also told that they are spiritually pure and will do the will of God regardless of negative consequences. They are considered by God to be *"firstfruits."* This means that there will be other Jewish people that will put faith and trust in their Messiah (Rom.11:26). It is also worth noting that their speech will be fully submitted to the Holy Spirit's leadership. The Spirit's testimony about them is that they are an unusually consecrated group of young people (Ja.1:26; 3:5-8). They will speak the whole counsel of God and will freely sacrifice their lives for the Gospel (Rev.7:9-17). They will go wherever the Lord sends them and speak whatever He tells them. It appears that their ministry influence is global and not simply confined to the nation of Israel. They will be wholehearted lovers of God and will certainly be on the Antichrist's most wanted list.

The Two Witnesses
(Please read to be familiar with the story line)

Then I was given a reed like a measuring rod. And the angel stood, saying, Rise and measure the temple of God, [the Jewish Tribulation Temple] the altar, and those who worship there [apparently the two witnesses were numbered among these worshippers]. (2) But leave out the court which is outside the temple, and do not measure it, for it has been given to the Gentiles. And they will tread the holy city underfoot for forty-two months [three-and-a-half years or Great Tribulation time frame]. (3) And I will give power to my two witnesses, and they will prophesy one thousand two hundred and sixty days [three- and-a-half years], clothed in sackcloth." (4) These are the two olive trees and the two lampstands standing before the God of the earth. (5) And if anyone wants to harm them, fire proceeds from their mouth [this is the impact of God's prophetic word in action] and devours their enemies. And if anyone wants to harm them, he must be killed in this manner. (6) These have power to shut heaven, so that no rain falls in the days of their prophecy; and they have power over waters to turn them to blood, and to strike the earth with all plagues, as often as they desire. (7) When they finish their testimony, the beast [the Antichrist] that ascends out of the bottomless pit will make war against them, overcome them, and kill them. (8) And their dead bodies will lie in the street of the great city which spiritually is called Sodom and Egypt, where also our Lord was crucified. (9) Then those from the peoples, tribes, tongues, and nations will see their dead bodies three-and-a-half days, and not allow their dead bodies to be put into graves. (10) And those who dwell on the earth will rejoice over them, make merry, and send gifts to one another, because these two prophets tormented those who dwell on the earth. (11) Now after the three-and-a-half days the breath of life from God entered them, and they stood on their feet, and great fear fell on those who saw them. (12) And they heard a loud voice from heaven saying to them, "Come up here." And they ascended to heaven in a cloud, and their enemies saw them. (13) In the same hour there was a great earthquake, and a tenth of

> *the city fell. In the earthquake seven thousand*
> *people were killed, and the rest were afraid and*
> *gave glory to the God of heaven*
> *(Rev.11:1-13)*

As a young Believer, when I first began reading about these *two witnesses* I was totally mystified and intrigued. These were like super heroes in my mind and seemed to appear just when things got really dark and troublesome.

There has been so much speculation about the identity of these two end time prophets that we could get side-tracked and devote an entire chapter on that subject alone. For the sake of time and sanity I will refrain and will leave the task of identification to other spiritual CSI investigators. Although many believe them to be resurrected Old Testament saints, that sounds more like New Age then it does New Testament (Heb.9:27). I believe that when the Bible is silent, then it is silent on purpose and we would be wise to follow suit.

So what is the primary function of these *two witnesses*? I think their very title tells us volumes. Their primary purpose is to give credible witness to the glory and majesty of the Son of God. Witnesses are people who have seen something compelling and are called upon to share that information with others. Witnesses can only be effective if their personal character holds up to public scrutiny. You can be sure that the Antichrist will do everything in his power to smear and spread false rumors about these witnesses in order to minimize their ministry effectiveness. His attempts to discredit them will fail and he will be forced to deal with their presence for most of the

Tribulation Period. This will prove to be a great embarrassment.

The connection between verse three and the first two verses makes it clear that these witnesses were associated with the temple and its worship before it became defiled by this evil world dictator. The portrayal of them being clothed with sackcloth indicates the deep level of spiritual defilement that has taken place by this Gentile ruler. The prophet Zechariah identified them as, *"These are the two anointed ones, who stand beside the Lord of the whole earth"* (Zech 4:14).

Like the prophet Elijah, if anyone attempts to harm them in any way, they will prophecy and pronounce God's judgment. Those who try to oppose them will instantly experience God's justice in an immediate and tangible way.

So, on the one hand you have the False Prophet calling down fire from heaven. Then, operating during the same period of time, you have an authentic demonstration of divine power. The problem this creates is that to the undiscerning spirit, both look similar and they both produce the same deadly results. So, what is going on here?

> *The coming of the lawless one is according to the working of Satan, with all power, signs, and lying wonders, (10) and with all unrighteous deception among those who perish, because they did not receive the love of the truth, that they might be saved. (11) And for this reason God will send them strong delusion, that they should believe the lie, (12) that they all may be condemned who did not believe the truth but had pleasure in unrighteousness (2 Thess.2:9-12).*

What we see happening here is the righteous administration of God's justice upon individuals who, through the operation of free will, have chosen to stand on the side of lawlessness rather than opening their hearts and accepting truth. They clearly overrule both their conscience and the conviction of the Holy Spirit. God therefore holds them accountable for that decision and will authorize the release of satanic counterfeit signs and wonders.

This should serve as a clear warning for anyone who has received past truth and revelation about God and is currently walking in hidden or open areas of darkness. Your choice of yielding to carnal desires may lead you to places that will remove you from access to God's presence. Now is the time to deal with the *"little foxes"* that are destroying your vine (SS. 2:15).

These two prophets will have the power to speak and cause entire regions to experience drought. It is possible that some areas may lack moisture for the entire forty-two months that they are permitted to prophesy. They, like Moses, will turn rivers into blood and are granted authority to produce any sort of plague or calamity they desire. These are not two guys you want to upset. They are two of God's counter-balances for exposing and dealing with the evil generation that will feel emboldened to do great acts of wickedness during this time. Jesus' testimony about this last day generation is equally alarming.

> *But as the days of Noah were, so also will the coming of the Son of Man be. (38) For as in the days before the flood, they were eating and drinking, marrying and giving in marriage, until the day that Noah entered the ark, (39) and did not know until the flood*

*came and took them all away, so also will the
coming of the Son of Man be
(Matt.24:37-39)*

These *Two Witnesses* will eventually be slain by the
Antichrist and their dead bodies will lie in the streets of
Jerusalem for a full three-and-a-half days. The entire world
will watch and will openly celebrate their death. The fact
that the city of Jerusalem is spiritually linked to both
Sodom and Egypt (Rev.11:8) tells volumes of what is
happening in the hearts of its citizens. Verse 10 makes it
clear that most people will be bound in darkness and will
have learned little during the ministry of these two
witnesses (Isa.60:1-2). Instead of mourning over their sin
they will be celebrating the restraints of God's judgments
being lifted.

Suddenly, during their impromptu holiday with all
its festivities, God will speak from heaven and cause the
two prophets to arise. They will be quickly transported to
heaven while a traumatized world looks on in disbelief.
This event will most likely be caught on live video tape and
be broadcast globally via satellite. I'm sure this will present
a formidable challenge for the Antichrist and his spin-
doctors to explain.

The earthquake that follows immediately after this
public resurrection will make these events extremely
difficult to cover-up. Seven thousand will perish in this
devastating quake and over one-tenth of the city will totally
collapse. Miraculously, many will be terrified and turn to
the Lord.

As you can see, these *two witnesses* play an
essential role in God's end time strategic plans. They will
operate with a similar anointing as the prophet Elijah.

The Mark of the Beast

He [The False Prophet] was granted power to give breath to the image of the beast [the image of the Antichrist], that the image of the beast should both speak and cause as many as would not worship the image of the beast to be killed. (16) He causes all, both small and great, rich and poor, free and slave, to receive a mark on their right hand or on their foreheads, (17) and that no one may buy or sell except one who has the mark or the name of the beast, or the number of his name
(Rev.13:15-17)

This is probably one of the most well-known last day scenarios in the entire Book of Revelation. More speculation and amateur conspiracies have emerged from these verses than time would allow us to pursue. Most of the attempts to identify the Antichrist revolve around the number 666 that is offered in verse eighteen of this passage. I have been a Christian for over thirty-five years and have seen an extensive list of impressive candidates that have been submitted by earnest Christian researchers in their quest to unmask this wicked man of sin. Using their mastery of the Greek and Hebrew languages, along with elaborate mathematical equations, combined with an over active imagination, these researchers seem to have an endless supply of names. To date, all of these contenders have fallen short and so the quest continues.

My point here is not to belittle earnest scholarship but rather to urge us to trust God with the timing of this unveiling. If it takes mastering foreign languages, higher math and secret formulas to reach a conclusion, I submit that this is not God's intent. The Lord will not allow His people to be deceived. In addition, the Antichrist will be nearly impossible to mistake for any Believer with a fiery heart, a thimble full of discernment and even an elementary understanding of biblical prophecy. So rest assured, God will reveal exactly what needs to be revealed, precisely when it needs to be revealed (Amos 3:7).

Unfortunately, it seems that most of the church's energy, interest and attention has been conveniently diverted not only in the wrong place, but also on the wrong event. "What do you mean? Isn't it important to know about this mark so we don't become needless targets because of ignorance?" someone might ask. Yes, biblical ignorance can certainly be costly. But when Believers focus their attention on the *Mark of the Beast*, they are putting their attention in the wrong place. Instead of looking at the wrong mark, they should refocus on the right mark. "Right mark, what do you mean? I thought there was only one mark handed out during the Tribulation? What's the other mark about, and who gets it?" The best way to avoid the *Mark of the Beast* in chapter thirteen is by receiving the *Seal of God* in chapter seven.

> *Do not harm the earth, the sea, or the trees*
> *till we have sealed the servants of our God*
> *on their foreheads*
> *(Rev.7:3)*
>
> *They were commanded not to harm the grass*
> *of the earth, or any green thing, or any tree,*

> *but only those men who do not have the seal*
> *of God on their foreheads*
> *(Rev.9:4)*

While all kinds of strange plagues and calamities are sweeping the globe and producing great pain and confusion, God will be supernaturally working to protect and provide for His people. It will be a repeat of what He did while His people were living in Egypt. He struck the entire nation with life threatening calamities, while His people living in Goshen experienced an amazing sense of peace and divine protection (Ex.8:22; 9:26). The promises of Psalm 91 will be the primary testimony of the Believers in those difficult times.

It appears that the False Prophet is the primary initiator of the *"Mark of the Beast"* (Rev.13:14-17). The sentence for noncompliance is death. There will be a strong spirit of intimidation and fear released as Christians get swept up in the drama of how to respond to this crisis. For many, this will present a real crisis of faith. Remember, to refuse the mark, in addition to capitol punishment, means no income, no access to public schools, no home ownership and no means to purchase food, gas or other basic necessities. In short, only those who are totally prepared to face martyrdom will be spiritually ready to refuse the mark. Do you catch the gravity of this situation? How many Christian families do you know today that are strong enough in the faith to trust God in the coming crisis?

I was recently with a mature Christian couple who serve in a leadership position with a nationally esteemed Christian ministry and our conversation drifted into talking about the last days. The wife brought up the subject about receiving the mark of the beast and then followed by giving her opinion about the matter. She sincerely believes that God will have mercy on Christians who yield to receiving the mark because they have families and need to have a means of supporting them. She said, *"God knows their hearts. If they truly love Him in their hearts and take the mark only as a means of provision for their families, surely God will forgive and keep them."*

If that statement seems right to you, then please pay close attention to what I have to say as it could literally be a matter of life and death both physically and spiritually for people you know. This is not an understatement. This is also not an issue that God is floating to see how popular it is with today's church. This is an issue that every Believer alive today would be wise to resolve in their heart now. You don't start building arks once it starts raining. Please read the following portion of scripture and see if you find any encouragement to attempt to negotiate with God over this matter.

> *If anyone worships the beast and his image [all who receive the mark are considered Beast worshippers], and receives his mark on his forehead or on his hand, (10) he himself [those individuals] shall also drink of the wine of the wrath of God, which is poured out full strength [self-explanatory] into the cup of His indignation. He shall be tormented with fire [sentenced to the Lake of Fire] and brimstone in the presence of the holy angels and in the presence of the Lamb. (11) And the smoke of their torment ascends forever and ever; and they have no rest day or night, who worship the beast and his*

> *image, and whoever [no distinction or*
> *special grace for those with "good hearts"*
> *and really love their families] receives the*
> *mark of his name*
> *(Rev.14:9-11)*

For those who are using the "love your family" option, I encourage you to think it all the way through. Does sending your entire family to the *Lake of Fire* forever qualify as "loving your family?" The time to make decisions on this matter is now, not later. Now is the time to start building a foundation of faith that is Bible-based and that withstands the pressures of that coming day. Only those who have built a mansion on the inside will be able to withstand the pressure coming on the outside. You don't wait until the day before you run the Boston Marathon to start training. I'd strongly suggest you start your spiritual preparations now.

I am on a mission to ensure that my entire family is totally ready to surrender their lives for Jesus Christ if called upon to do so. There should be absolutely no other alternative for the sincere Believer besides heeding the Word of the Lord in this matter. I do not consider the *Lake of Fire* a viable option for anyone who names the name of Jesus as Lord. This is a serious crisis and every Believer needs to decide *now* how he will respond.

Who Will Refuse the Mark?

There will be basically two categories of individuals who will absolutely choose to face the uncertainty of hardship, and if necessary, death, rather than yield to the False Prophet's demand for compliance. There is ample evidence in history to substantiate that these two groups have always risen to the occasion and therefore there is no reason to assume that this period of time will find them any less determined to resist tyranny.

The first group is those who love Jesus more than their own lives (Rev.12:10). The second group is the resisters. These are individuals who choose non-compliance for reasons other than religious convictions. Many are rugged individualists who refuse the authority of a rogue dictator. They will deeply resent the Antichrist and will refuse to comply as a matter of principle. They will prefer living off the land and chose total seclusion to bending their knee to a world leader whom they deeply resent. They will discern his false motives and see through his peaceful facade. Many of these resisters will come to faith during the Great Tribulation. I firmly believe that there will be multiplied millions of this type of individual worldwide.

The Bible is clear that the times of the last days will come upon us suddenly and will catch many off guard (1 Thess.5:3). There will be a mass defection from the faith as many carnal Christians yield to the pressure of the Antichrist rather than trusting in the Lord to sustain them (2 Thess.2:3). This time of crisis is fast approaching and I encourage every Believer to take a deep spiritual inventory and ask the Holy Spirit what you need to do to prepare your heart for the coming firestorm.

> *Examine yourselves as to whether you are in the faith. Test yourselves. Do you not know yourselves, that Jesus Christ is in you? -- unless indeed you are disqualified. (6) But I trust that you will know that we are not disqualified (2 Cor.13:5-6).*

Because you have kept My command to persevere, I also will keep you from the hour of trial which shall come upon the whole world, to test those who dwell on the earth. (11) Behold, I am coming quickly! Hold fast what you have, that no one may take your crown (Rev.3:10-11).

CHAPTER 13

God's End of the Age Final Exam

One of the major issues that the Holy Spirit is beginning to confront within the Gentile church today concerns our relationship to the Jewish people. This will be one of the Gentile church's greatest challenges in days to come. When was the last time you heard a message taught on God's jealous love for the people of Israel (Zech. 1:14; 8:2)? That's just what I suspected. There aren't many teachings available on that subject. This is an area in which most Christians have received little or no instruction. What if I were to tell you that the church's relationship with the Jewish people will become a high priority item on God's end time agenda? Would you find that statement believable? What if I were to take it up a notch and tell you that the church's treatment of the Jewish people will directly impact their relationship with God. Could you receive that?

These next verses will be of foremost significance in the near future. They are not intended for the timid, the undiscerning or those who are closed-minded to progressive revelation. I have found these verses to either offend or to inspire, depending on the quality of the soil of the heart upon which they fall. Some of the strongest words breathed by the Holy Spirit and recorded in the New Testament were warnings given to the Gentile church as it regards her treatment of the Jewish people. As you read, ask yourself this question, "Has the Gentile church followed the Holy Spirit's instruction in this matter?" I have inserted comments to help clarify.

I say then, have they [the Jewish people] stumbled that they should fall [be disqualified to receive the blessings of God]? Certainly not! But through their fall, to provoke them [the Jewish people] to jealousy, salvation has come to the Gentiles. (12) Now if their fall is riches for the world [massive numbers of Gentiles coming to faith], and their failure riches for the Gentiles, how much more their fullness [what will it look like when God pours out His Spirit on the Jews again] (Rom.11:11-12)

And if some of the branches were broken off [God's judicial dealings with His people], and you, being a wild olive tree [not part of the original covenant], were grafted in among them, and with them became a partaker of the root and fatness of the olive tree [because of Christ's sacrifice, Gentiles have been given equal access to the Father], (18) do not boast against the branches [don't mistake God's kindness as a sign of favored status and get a prideful spirit]. But if you do boast, remember that you do not support the root, but the root supports you. (19) You will say then, "Branches were broken off that I might be grafted in." (20) Well said. Because of unbelief they were broken off, and you stand by faith. Do not be haughty [keep a watch on your attitude], but fear. (21) For if

God did not spare the natural branches, He may not spare you either. (22) Therefore consider the goodness and severity of God: on those who fell, severity; but toward you, goodness, if you continue in His goodness. Otherwise you also will be cut off [if we mistreat the Jewish people who are currently struggling under the weight of God's justice, God just may put us under severe discipline as well]
(Rom.11:17-22)

For I do not desire, brethren, that you [Gentiles] should be ignorant of this mystery [a hidden truth now made plain through a spirit of revelation], lest you should be wise in your own opinion [reject God's instruction on this subject], that blindness in part has happened to Israel until the fullness of the Gentiles [this is both the full number and the fullness of last day power and anointing] has come in [this number will not be complete until the Antichrist – the last Gentile ruler – is completely subdued by Jesus at His Second Coming]. (26) And so all Israel will be saved [the Jewish remnant alive when Jesus returns will be suddenly converted – (Zech. 12:10)]
(Rom.11:25-26)

The Gentile church has been given a strong end time mandate by God to love His covenant people and to provoke them into the Kingdom of God by love and good

173

deeds. Let me show you how serious God is about this mandate.

Baffled

There is a passage that for many years baffled me. Every time I heard it mentioned in conversation or referenced during a teaching, it was always put in the context of outreach to the poor. I understand the principles involved and agree that this text certainly carries with it application for reaching out to the poor, but that is clearly a secondary application. So what's the primary lesson? Read it and see if you can pick it out. Please understand that the context is the last days. Jesus began His end time seminar at the beginning of Mathew twenty-four and these words were a continuation of that teaching. In fact, He chose to conclude His instruction about the last days with these valuable insights: (underlines added for emphasis)

> *"When the Son of Man comes in His glory [Second Coming], and all the holy angels with Him, then He will sit on the throne of His glory. (32) All the nations will be gathered before Him, and He will separate them one from another, as a shepherd divides his sheep from the goats. (33) And He will set the sheep on His right hand, but the goats on the left. (34) Then the King will say to those on His right hand, 'Come, you blessed of My Father, inherit the kingdom prepared for you from the foundation of the world: (35) for I was **hungry** and you gave Me food; I was **thirsty** and you gave Me drink; I was a*

stranger and you took Me in; (36) I was naked and you clothed Me; I was sick and you visited Me; I was in prison and you came to Me. (37) "Then the righteous will answer Him, saying, 'Lord, when did we see You hungry and feed You, or thirsty and give You drink? (38) When did we see You a stranger and take You in, or naked and clothe You? (39) Or when did we see You sick, or in prison, and come to You?' (40) And the King will answer and say to them, 'Assuredly, I say to you, inasmuch as you did it to one of the least of these My brethren, you did it to Me
(Matt. 25:31-40)

The story Jesus is relating is both simple to follow and clear in its meaning. When Jesus returns there is going to be both a separation and an evaluation. He gathers one group and puts it here, then gathers another group and places it there. That's the separation part. So now we have two groups gathered and standing in two separate locations. The group on His right He identifies as sheep and the ones on His left He calls goats.

Six Basic Needs

After the separation the evaluation begins. Individuals are evaluated based on how they responded to six basic human needs. The six needs are as follows: (1) hunger (2) thirst (3) housing (4) clothing (5) sickness and (6) imprisonment. These are not difficult needs to meet and require no special skills. The only thing necessary to meet these needs is godly compassion. Unsaved people meet these kinds of needs everyday. This does not require a high level of spiritual maturity and is *"doable"* for the newest Believer.

The Pop Quiz

So here is the problem I struggled with for years as a pastor. Knowing that these are really simple needs, why does Jesus select these needs as His standard by which to evaluate His people? What is happening here seems to be the equivalent of a huge pop quiz that is given, by Jesus, at the end of the age. The good news is that the final exam only contains six questions. The scary thing is that your score determines whether you pass or fail the course. There are no extra credits, nor does this professor grade on a curve. How you respond to these six needs seems to be Jesus' primary concern. Are you catching my point? We will be separated and identified as either *"sheep"* or *"goats"* depending on how we responded to these basic needs. Are you still with me?

You'd think, if this is the end-of-the-age final exam, one might assume that Jesus would be asking some really complex theological questions to see if we applied ourselves to studying His Word. Or that He would gather all the church attendance records and evaluate our faithfulness in showing up for meetings. However, Jesus seems more interested in how we participated in meeting human needs than anything else.

As I tried to evaluate these verses in the light of what I'd always heard or been taught, I became even more confused and perplexed. Surely Jesus is not going to separate Believers based solely on whether they showed up for outreach to the poor. I'm sure that will matter in the larger scheme of things but that can't be the primary determining factor. What about the individuals who were unable to participate in the prison ministry because they worked a swing shift and were responsible to meet the needs of their families? Surely Jesus wouldn't fault them for being a good provider? How about the families with four kids who are pressed for space because they live in a small mobile home? Would Jesus penalize them because they didn't have room to take in the stranger? Do you see my problem?

Knowing the kindness of the Lord and how He understands human needs, His apparent harshness was troubling. I knew in my spirit that something more was going on here because this matter was inconsistent with everything else I knew and understood about Jesus. But what was it? Why was Jesus so focused on these six concerns? Would He really reward or punish people based primarily on how they responded to these circumstances?

Understanding the Qualifier

I discovered the key when I understood two things. First, the context was the last days. The second had to do with understanding the qualifier. So what was the qualifier? The qualifier involves understanding not only _what_ was being done but _who_ was being affected. The *"what"* were the six human needs. The *"who"* are specifically the Jewish people. Jesus referred to them as *"The least of these my brethren"* (Matt.25:40). The better literal translation would be *"The least of these my Jewish brethren."* Most Gentiles don't catch this because we have been raised with such a consistent dose of low grade replacement theology that we

177

arrogantly presuppose the entire Bible is all about us. One of the key titles attributed to God throughout the Bible is, *"The Lord God of Israel"* (Jos.10:40).

Here's what is happening. After discussing the extraordinary events of the last days (Matt. 24), Jesus opens Matthew twenty-five by mentioning two parables that address issues of intimacy, (the ten virgins) and faithfulness, (talents). Then suddenly he shifts from intimacy and faithfulness and begins discussing mercy deeds.

What's happening here is this. After the Antichrist desecrates the Jewish Temple in Jerusalem, (i.e. *"The Abomination of Desolation"*) he will immediately begin his diabolical plan to wipe out every single Jewish person on the planet. He will attempt to finish what Adolf Hitler started. Remember, his ultimate goal is to stay out of prison and avoid the *"Lake of Fire,"* and he intends to accomplish that by exploiting the biblical loophole (Matt.24:37) that we discussed earlier.

God Intervenes to Save the Jewish People

God has two methods of intervention that He will employ in order to save a Jewish remnant and prepare it for His Second Coming. The first is sovereign and becomes extremely frustrating to Satan which causes him to elevate and refocus his rage (Rev.12:13-17). The Bible identifies the target of his anger as *"The rest of her offspring"* which has a Jewish and non-Jewish component. Although God's direct intervention allows many Jews to flee into the wilderness where they are concealed through supernatural means (Rev.12:13-17), at the same time there are Jews that are left unprotected and become targets of the devil's wrath through his puppet ruler, the Antichrist (Zech.13:8). Also considered part of this offspring are those in covenant with God or Gentile Believers who have refused to take the Mark of the Beast. They will be equally hated and hunted.

God's second method of intervention is through a compassionate Gentile church that has been given revelation about God's heart for the Jewish people. I learned a long time ago if you want to operate under God's blessing, find out what He loves and pursue it. Find out what He hates and avoid it. God has a passionate desire for Israel (Isa.49:16) and it is revealed everywhere you turn in scripture.

Gentile Intervention

During the season when the Antichrist is focused on executing every Jewish person alive on the planet, the Gentile church will be God's primary instrument of concealment. Although the church in Europe did a dreadful job of assisting the Jews who were fleeing for their lives during World War II, we will be given another opportunity and God will provide supernatural means for those who get involved.

This is the focus of the Matthew twenty-five text and now you can understand why Jesus is so passionate that *"His brethren"* are not forsaken. What would you do for someone who took care of your family in a time of great crisis? What would you do to someone who could have easily assisted your family in a serious crisis and willfully chose not to get involved? That is exactly what is happening in Matthew twenty-five, verses thirty-one through forty-six. The consequences for anyone, including Gentile Believers, who refuse to get involved will be

179

horrific - *"And these will go away into everlasting punishment, but the righteous into eternal life" (Matt.25:4).* Jesus makes it clear that this matter is not to be taken lightly but with a sober spirit.

So, how do we obtain a heart for the Jewish people? The best way I know is to commit to pray for them regularly. I have discovered that the people you pray for are the ones with whom you end up falling in love. You will receive a token of God's compassion for them as well.

I appeal to the Gentile church to consider this matter with a prayerful spirit. Meditate on this passage and I believe you will conclude that Jesus is attempting to awaken a sleepy Gentile church to join Him in loving and praying for the Jewish people (Rom.8:34).

CHAPTER 14

The Woman and the Dragon

*Therefore when you see the 'abomination of
desolation,' spoken of by Daniel the prophet,
standing in the holy place" [whoever reads,
let him understand], (16) "then let those who
are in Judea flee to the mountains. (17) Let
him who is on the housetop not go down to
take anything out of his house. (18) And let
him who is in the field not go back to get his
clothes. (19) But woe to those who are
pregnant and to those who are nursing
babies in those days! (20) And pray that your
flight may not be in winter or on the Sabbath.
(21) For then there will be great tribulation,
such as has not been since the beginning of
the world until this time, no, nor ever shall
be. (22) And unless those days were
shortened, no flesh would be saved; but for
the elect's sake those days will be shortened.
(Matt.24:15-22)*

God's Most Overlooked Intercessory Invitation

Jesus' warning here will be a matter of life or death
depending on the response of those Jews who are living in
Israel when this event takes place. Notice the urgency to act
quickly and decisively. The individuals who hesitate, like
Lot's wife, will suffer serious consequences. We are

invited to pray into this circumstance and appeal to the Lord for mercy. I personally believe that if the church responds and prays that God might change the season and allow this event to happen in the spring or fall rather than when it would be most difficult, in winter (cold) or summer (hot).

Jesus makes it plain that *"The abomination of desolation"* will be the starting point of unparalleled persecution for the Jewish people. The entire earth will be impacted by God's judgments. This is the time the Bible calls *"The Great Tribulation."* This season of time will impact and test every single person on earth. Men will make clear decisions as to where their spiritual allegiance lies. This will be an hour of declaration. There will be only two choices. Men will either choose to serve Jesus and face temporal (negative) consequences or will choose to serve the Antichrist and face eternal (really negative) consequences.

Last Day Events

During this time, which will last three-and-a-half years, many critical events will be happening. Some will run simultaneously. God will be releasing twenty-one numbered judgments. Each of these will have considerable global, as well as profound regional consequences. The False Prophet will be calling down fire from heaven, deceiving the entire earth and doing what the Bible terms, *"Lying signs and wonders"* (Rev.13:13). The Two Witnesses will be prophesying, as well as causing global droughts and doing whatever signs and wonders they desire (Rev.11:6). True Believers will be operating at a level of spiritual power as never before in history, doing more remarkable signs than Jesus preformed (Jn.14:12). More saints will suffer martyrdom than at any other time in church history (Rev.13:7-8). The most wicked nation on earth, Babylon, will be quickly established and soon destroyed in a swift and comprehensive display of God's wrath (Rev.18:2,10). The nations will be gathered against Jerusalem and will also experience the overwhelming judgment of God (Joel 3:2).

As you can tell from this list of terrifying events, Jesus was not overstating things when He forecasted the last days to be the most troublesome times ever since the beginning of mankind (Matt.24:21).

The Devil's Ploy to Avoid Incarceration

As we have stated earlier, the devil will be fighting for his survival. His goal is to prevent the Second Coming of Jesus Christ (1 Thess.4:16-17). If he is successful, then he will avoid a trip to the Bottomless Pit (Rev.20:3) and also to his ultimate incarceration in the *Lake of Fire* (Rev.20:10). In order to avoid being imprisoned by God he must wipe out the Jewish race. They are the only people who have been given both the mandate and the authority to welcome Jesus, their Jewish Messiah, back to plant earth. In order to fulfill the prophetic decree (Matt.23:37) several things must happen. There must be a Jewish remnant that is alive and living in Jerusalem that reaches a united consensus that Jesus (Yeshua) truly is their long awaited Messiah.

The Book of Revelation gives us a rare glimpse behind the scenes of what is actually taking place in the spirit realm and how it impacts the drama unfolding on the earth at the end of the age. Because the Bible describes these events by using an unusual amount of symbolic language, I will try to make this portion of scripture easier for the reader by inserting phrases that should clarify what is being communicated. I think you will find that these verses contain some of the most extraordinary insights in the Bible.

Now a great sign appeared in heaven: a woman [Israel / Jewish remnant] ... (2) Then being with child (Jesus), she cried out in labor and in pain to give birth. (3) And another sign appeared in heaven: behold, a great, fiery red dragon [Satan] ... (4) His tail drew a third of the stars [1/3rd of angels] of heaven and threw them to the earth [became demonic spirits]. And the dragon [Satan] stood ... to devour her Child [Jesus] ... (5) who was to rule all nations with a rod of iron [Millennial Kingdom]. And her Child [Jesus] was caught up to God [crucified, resurrected, and ascended] and His throne. (6) [Story line suddenly shifts to last days] Then the woman [Israel/Jewish remnant] fled into the wilderness [after the abomination of desolation], where she has a place prepared by God [supernatural protection], that they [angelic assistance] should feed her there one thousand two hundred and sixty days [last half of the Tribulation Period]. (7) And war broke out in heaven ... (9) So the great dragon [Satan] was cast out [expelled], that serpent of old, called the Devil and Satan, who deceives the whole world [his agents for deception will be the Antichrist and the False Prophet]; he [Satan] was cast to the earth, and his angels [demons] were cast out with him ... (12) Therefore rejoice, O heavens, and you who dwell in them! Woe to the inhabitants of the earth and the sea! For the devil has come down to you, having great wrath, because he knows that he has a short time." (13) Now when the dragon [Satan] saw that he had been cast to the earth, he persecuted the woman [Israel/Jewish remnant] ... (14) was given two wings of a great eagle [supernatural speed to escape to safety], that she might fly into the wilderness [probably Judean desert] to her place [place of supernatural protection], where she is nourished [supernatural provision] for a time and times and half a time [3 ½ yrs.], from the presence of the serpent [Satan]. (15) So the serpent [Satan] spewed water out of his mouth like a flood [a supernatural attempt to kill Jewish remnant] ... (16) But the earth helped the woman [God protected the Jewish remnant], and the earth opened its mouth and swallowed up the flood which the dragon had spewed out of his mouth. (17) And the dragon [Satan] was enraged with the woman [Israel / Jewish remnant], and he went to make war [severe persecution] with the rest of her offspring [Jewish remnant who didn't flee plus the Gentile Believers],

> *who keep the commandments of God and*
> *have the testimony of Jesus*
> *(Rev.12:1-7,9,12-17)*

As this end time snapshot clearly demonstrates, the devil will be unleashing unprecedented resources in order to completely eradicate the Jewish race and *"The rest of her offspring,"* which are Gentile Believers. After the Antichrist forcefully takes control of the newly constructed Jewish Temple, his plans for the execution of every Jewish person, as well as every follower of Jesus, will soon be manifest on a global scale. The destiny of the Jewish people and the Gentile church are intrinsically bound together forever in God's elaborate redemptive plan. The sooner the Gentile church understands this, the sooner we can line up with God's awesome last day purposes. Let me show you one facet of the Gentile church's end time assignment, as it relates to the Jewish people:

> *I [God)] have set watchmen [Gentile intercessors] on your walls, O Jerusalem; they shall never hold their peace day or night [will fulfill the mandate to pray around the clock]. You who make mention of the LORD, do not keep silent [God's charge to the Gentile church] (7) and give Him no rest till He establishes and till He makes Jerusalem a praise in the earth [the job will not be considered finished until the Jewish people recognize and receive their Messiah – Jesus – as Lord]*
> *(Isa.62:6-7)*

One of the great surprises in the last days will be the energy and commitment the church will have in focusing much of its prayer strategies upon the Jewish remnant. Unfortunately, this is not on most of today's churches' radar screens. In fact, praying for Israel is a great oddity in most prayer circles but there is a fresh wind of revelation and unction beginning to blow.

The End Time Prayer Movement

In the early eighties, there was a sovereign prophetic charge given to the Gentile church by the audible voice of the Lord. Some have referred to this call as the *"Israel Mandate."* Mike Bickle, the senior leader of the International House of Prayer (IHOP), received multiple prophetic words, visions and remarkable supernatural signs that confirmed God's intentions to raise-up an end time army of intercessors. The primary target of this prayer movement would be the nation of Israel and specifically the salvation of Jewish souls. The surprising twist to this whole scenario was that most of the intercessors would be teenagers and young people in their early twenties. This intercessory prayer movement was given the charge to fast and pray, day and night, until the Lord returns.

Although IHOP in Kansas City has been faithfully responding to that call for many years, multiple groups across the nation have also been receiving their own mandate to gather and pray for Israel as well. This same charge has been issued throughout the nations and is spreading on a much larger scale internationally. Even though this emphasis to pray for the Jewish people is in its infancy, there seems to be real momentum building and as a result, Israel is experiencing astounding spiritual

187

breakthroughs. While the prayer movement is in its mustard seed form today (Mark 4:30-32), like the parable of the kingdom, it will soon spread and cover the entire earth.

CHAPTER 15

The Second Coming

But I do not want you to be ignorant, brethren, concerning those who have fallen asleep, lest you sorrow as others who have no hope. (14) For if we believe that Jesus died and rose again, even so God will bring with Him those who sleep in Jesus. (15) For this we say to you by the word of the Lord, that we who are alive and remain until the coming of the Lord will by no means precede those who are asleep. (16) For the Lord Himself will descend from heaven with a shout, with the voice of an archangel, and with the trumpet of God. And the dead in Christ will rise first. (17) Then we who are alive and remain shall be caught up together with them in the clouds to meet the Lord in the air. And thus we shall always be with the Lord. (18) Therefore comfort one another with these words
(1 Thess.4:13-18)

The most anticipated end time event for Christians, without question, is the *Second Coming of Jesus Christ*. No single episode in scripture has engendered more passionate debate and has been open to more speculation than that which regards *"His Appearing"* (2 Tim.4:8) at the end of the age. Although there is strong support among almost all

Believers that the *Second Coming* is a well established biblical fact, most of the controversy centers on the timing of His coming.

Why All the Confusion?

Part of the reason for the confusion is because little is done to separate what is commonly called the *Rapture* from the *Second Coming*. Most Believers have never really thought this through and thus have viewed the Rapture and the Second Coming as one event. Nothing could be further from the truth. I believe you will find this chapter helpful in sorting through the differences of these two entirely different events.

The primary difference between them is: (1) the Rapture deals with what happens to the church when Jesus comes and (2) the Second Coming deals with what Jesus does when He returns. Both of these events occur during what some call the *Second Coming Procession*. An important point for us to understand is that there is a clear distinction between Jesus' coming and His appearing in the sky. *"His appearing"* is relatively brief, while *"His Coming"* is for eternity.

The Bible refers to the *Second Coming* as our *"Blessed hope"* (Titus 2:13) and the New Testament mentions this event over three hundred times. There is more attention given to this subject than any other event in the entire Bible. Rather than struggle from a lack of information, we must instead wrestle with information-overload.

The word *Rapture*, although not found in the Bible, comes from a Latin word which means, *"to catch up"* or *"to snatch away."* This word is used to describe the event mentioned in several key New Testament passages.

> *Then we who are alive and remain shall be* **caught up** *together with them in the clouds to meet the Lord in the air. And thus we shall always be with the Lord*
> *(1 Thess.4:17)*

> *Behold, I tell you a mystery: We shall not all sleep, but we shall* **all be changed** *– (52)* **in a moment**, *in the twinkling of an eye,* **at the last trumpet**. *For the trumpet will sound, and the dead will be raised incorruptible, and we shall be changed*
> *(1 Cor.15:51-52)*

It is clear from both of these texts that there will be a group of Believers alive on earth when the Lord returns. Jesus used the phrase, *"Those who endure to the end"* (Matt.24:13) when referencing this same group. I find it difficult to justify a pre-tribulation removal when the weight of scripture on this subject instructs us to persevere through the time of tribulation. Why else would Jesus have mentioned specifically those who *"Endure to the end"* if He understood that the church would be removed at the beginning? If you *"endure"* something, that word indicates that someone has gone through an extremely difficult circumstance. Even though the Great Tribulation only lasts three-and-a-half years, it will be the most trying time ever for those who live through it.

The Last Trumpet

The mystery that Paul refers to in 1 Corinthians 15:51 is not about when the rapture happens but rather what takes place during this amazing event. Paul plainly states that this catching away happens when the last trumpet is sounded. If we could discover when that happens then we could know for sure when the church might expect to be raptured, correct? The most effective and safest way to interpret the Word of God is to simply take what it says at face value. Does that make sense? In order for there to be a last trumpet, then it follows that there must be a first trumpet followed by a series of trumpet blasts. The Book of Revelation lists these trumpets in their chronological order with the last trumpet sounding in Revelation 11:15. As you read these accounts you will get a sense of what is taking place as well as the timing.

> *Then the seventh angel sounded: And there were loud voices in heaven, saying, the kingdoms of this world have become the kingdoms of our Lord and of His Christ, and He shall reign forever and ever!*
>
> *... in the days of the sounding of the seventh angel, when he is about to sound, **the mystery of God would be finished**, as He declared to His servants the prophets (Rev.10:7).*

As we mentioned earlier, the seven trumpets will follow the opening of the seven seals. The seven trumpets will be followed by the seven bowls of God's wrath. Just prior to those bowls being poured out, God removes His people. This is one of the last things to happen at the closing of this age and will certainly not occur at the beginning of the seven year Tribulation Period. How can we be sure? There are absolutely no trumpets sounding during the pre-tribulation timeframe, or at least there are none recorded in scripture. If you just let the Bible interpret itself on this matter you will see this is really a simple issue to understand. There are only seven trumpets that sound in the Book of Revelation and the seventh happens to be the last trumpet mentioned in scripture that is blown and heard. Therefore, it stands to reason that the seventh trumpet is synonymous with the last trumpet. Revelation 10:7 tells us that when this happens, the mystery of God is finished. If these verses were formatted and displayed in a movie theater, the credits would be rolling. Does that seem reasonable? You can't miss the Holy Spirit's obvious attempt to drive home the point that the sounding of the seventh trumpet marks the end of this current age. Doesn't that seem to be a fitting time for His people to join Him? This is not rocket science, but just taking what the Bible says in its simplest form. What happens next is really quite amazing.

> *Behold, I tell you a mystery: We shall not all sleep [experience death], but we shall all be changed [receive a glorified body] (52) in a moment, in the twinkling of an eye [1/100th of a second], at the last trumpet [seventh trumpet]. For the trumpet will sound, and the dead will be raised incorruptible, and we shall be changed*
> *(1 Cor.15:51-53)*

The one thing about this event that is unmistakable is when this change happens. Talk about the ultimate make-over. At the last trumpet our earthly bodies don't just get a face-lift or a tummy-tuck; rather, they literally become something from another age. The corruptible suddenly become incorruptible. The earthly instantly become heavenly. That which was sown in weakness is now raised in power. The weak can finally say, in a definitive way, *"I am strong"* (Joel 3:10).

> *Beloved, now we are children of God; and it has not yet been revealed what we shall be, but we know that when He is revealed [at the last trumpet and we have risen to meet Him in the air], we shall be like Him [we too will be given a glorified body] for we shall see Him as He is*
> *(1 John 3:2)*

Free At Last

What that will look like or feel like we can only imagine. To live in a body untouched and undefiled by sin is unfathomable because of our current weakened state. All sickness and disease will instantly be eradicated. Those with terminal illnesses will experience immediate restoration. The blind will see, the lame will walk, the deaf will hear for the first time. Those with missing limbs will have fully restored bodies. Depression will lift immediately and be replaced by a sound mind and a rejoicing spirit. Those carrying deep wounds and scars from abusive relationships will be caught up in the ecstatic joy of the

Lord. Pain, misery and brokenness of any kind will be instantly removed, never to return again. It will be like getting born-again for the first time but a thousand times more dynamic. Condemnation and shame for past short-comings will be taken away and never remembered. It will be like God pushes *"delete"* on everything that has ever defiled our spirit.

For a clearer picture of what will happen at this time, let's take a look at some verses that will put many of the final end time events in perspective.

> *Then the seventh angel sounded: And there were loud voices in heaven, saying, "The kingdoms of this world have become the kingdoms of our Lord and of His Christ, and He shall reign forever and ever!"* (16) *And the twenty-four elders who sat before God on their thrones fell on their faces and worshiped God,* (17) *saying: "We give You thanks, O Lord God Almighty, the one who is and who was and who is to come, because You have taken Your great power and reigned.* (18) *The nations were angry, and Your wrath has come, and the time of the dead, that they should be judged, and that You should reward Your servants the prophets and the saints, and those who fear Your name, small and great, and should destroy those who destroy the earth"*
> *(Rev.11:15-18)*

There are five critical things all happening about the same time or in close proximity of each other. First, the entire earth now comes under the righteous leadership of Jesus Christ. Secondly, the nations rage against His leadership and that hatred becomes fully manifest. Thirdly, the unrighteous dead will be judged, found guilty and sentenced to spend 1,000 years in Hades, a temporary holding cell. Then they join Satan and his angels in the Lake of Fire. Fourthly, the saints are rewarded. Finally, the rebellious still living on the earth will be destroyed as God pours out the final seven bowls of wrath.

The Second Coming Procession

Most Believers have never thought through exactly what the Second Coming Procession might look like. We have enough clues in scripture that when pasted together, they provide us with sufficient information to make a comprehensive observation of what is transpiring when Jesus returns. Let's look at some of these scriptures.

> *Behold, He is coming with clouds, and **every eye** will see Him, even they who pierced Him. And **all the tribes of the earth** will mourn because of Him. Even so, Amen (Rev.1:7)*

Please note what this verse actually says and then be aware of what we often assume it is saying. What does that mean? We imagine that somehow through supernatural intervention, the entire earth sees Jesus simultaneously. Obviously, the God of Genesis 1 can do anything He chooses and cannot be limited. However, as we will see more fully in the coming chapter, God appears to be working through natural processes, with a substantial increase of the supernatural dimensions, even during His Millennial reign.

Why am I saying this? Many assume that when Jesus returns, He will simply snap His fingers and everything immediately will change from one state of being to another. We also assume that just like our bodies were miraculously transformed in the blink of an eye, that all creation and everything on the planet will likewise experience an instant make-over. There is nothing in scripture that supports that theory as far as I can tell.

Paradigm Shift

Let me offer a new paradigm for you to consider when it comes to the Second Coming Procession. Two things that I believe will stun most people about this procession are: (1) the glory of this procession and (2) the length of time involved in completing this procession.

First, let's look at the glory of His Coming Procession. Try to visualize the incredible spectacle that is described in these verses. The glory is *"other-worldly."*

> *Jesus said to him, It is as you said. Nevertheless, I say to you, hereafter you will see the Son of Man sitting at the right hand of the Power, and coming on the clouds of heaven*
> *(Matt.26:64)*

> *For the Son of Man will come in the glory of His Father with His angels, and then He will reward each according to his works*
> *(Matt.16:27)*

> *Behold, the Lord comes with ten thousands*
> *of His saints*
> *(Jude 14b)*

> *Now I saw heaven opened, and behold, a*
> *white horse. And He who sat on him was*
> *called Faithful and True, and in*
> *righteousness He judges and makes war. (12)*
> *His eyes were like a flame of fire, and on His*
> *head were many crowns. He had a name*
> *written that no one knew except Himself. (13)*
> *He was clothed with a robe dipped in blood,*
> *and His name is called The Word of God. (14)*
> *And the armies in heaven, clothed in fine*
> *linen, white and clean, followed Him on*
> *white horses. (15) Now out of His mouth goes*
> *a sharp sword, that with it He should strike*
> *the nations. And He Himself will rule them*
> *with a rod of iron. He Himself treads the*
> *winepress of the fierceness and wrath of*
> *Almighty God. (16) And He has on His robe*
> *and on His thigh a name written: KING OF*
> *KINGS AND LORD OF LORDS*
> *(Rev.19:11-16)*

If you are thinking that the Second Coming of Jesus will look anything like His first coming you had better fasten your seat belt. There will be absolutely no comparison. What we saw of Him in His humanity will not even be remembered when we see Him in His glory. Everywhere you turn in the Book of Revelation you find people falling on their face in terror of this worthy King. The Apostle John was so traumatized that he started bowing before everything that moved (Rev.19:10). He was even gently rebuked for bowing before an angel. He was totally moved off-center at the realm of glory that surrounded this King of Kings and Lord of Lords. Although this was the same man who leaned on Jesus when He came the first time, when John saw Jesus in His glory, the only thought on his mind appeared to be, how low could he get?

Second Coming Procession

Check-out His Second Coming Procession. Leading the procession, seated on a white stallion is the one with eyes that appear to be on fire. We're talking focus. He is on a mission to completely subdue the earth that is still full of mockers, reprobates and enemies of righteousness. The earth is full of vile humans who became demonized when they received *"The mark of the beast."* They hate God and despise His Son and their hands are still freshly stained with the blood of innocent martyrs. They are getting ready to experience an act of violence that is unequalled by any Hollywood special effects movie. One big difference - this is for real and forever. These mockers misunderstood His delay in pouring out His justice as approval for their wicked deeds and they assumed He was soft on sin. However, this One leading the procession and sitting on His white war-horse is anything but timid and weak. His robe is stained with His own blood that He shed while purchasing salvation for any who would call upon His name. It is the last reminder to those who have scoffed at Him with their endless blasphemies and cursing. A last reminder that they could have experienced the bountiful kindness of His tender mercies but now their fate is sealed forever. The same robe that is covered with the costly blood of the King of Glory will stand as a witness against their ill-conceived rebellion. It will now serve as an omen of what they can expect for they will only know the full measure of His wrath.

Behind Him, also seated on white horses, are multiplied millions of righteous saints. Old Testament Believers join with New Testament saints to make up this spectacular procession. Their faces will be glowing with the supernatural aura which their new glorified bodies radiate. Each of them is clothed in a radiant white robe. This indicates the righteousness, which they graciously received, from the only one worthy and who is leading this spectacular display. Behind these trails a seemingly endless array of angels also dressed in dazzling white robes and seated on white horses. Nothing like this procession has ever been seen before nor will anything like it be witnessed again. This is literally a once-in-a-lifetime event.

Timing is Everything

The second thing about the Second Coming Procession that most Christians will find unusual is the time it takes to complete this march. This procession is not about showing off the new robes and displaying an endless sea of people and angelic hosts. This is a war procession. It is being led by a real King into a real battle. There is still work to be done in order to bring all things under the rule of this warrior King. The prophetic warnings of Psalm 2, as well as in many other places in scripture, have gone unheeded and the time of vengeance of our God has come.

Most of us have not given this whole procession idea much thought. Therefore, we have assumed that Jesus will simply appear in the sky for a moment, while an astounded world gawks in amazement. With mouths wide-open they will mutter in whispered tones and in unison, "Wow." Then the credits start rolling because the show is over. Most view this as the equivalent of a really spectacular photo-op and totally disconnect with what is actually happening.

Think about it for a moment. How does the whole world see Jesus all at one time? Is this some kind of high tech global conferencing deal going on here? Does the entire planet suddenly go flat for a few seconds so everybody gets a good look and then just as suddenly go back to normal? Does God momentarily increase the size of Jesus so he can be seen everywhere at once? How about the people on the other side of the globe? How do they see Him at the same time as the people who live multiple time zones away?

Let's Get Real

Let's take another approach for a moment. Let's pretend that God combines the use of supernatural means with natural processes. Jesus came to earth as a human and will probably return with the same size body and the same features as He had when on earth the first time. The big difference between His first and Second Coming will be the unmistakable majesty and splendor, which when revealed, will stagger the imaginations of both friend and foe alike.

Let's say Jesus was five foot ten inches tall when He came during His first advent. How high up in the air would He have to be so that the average person could see Him clearly enough to verify that this is truly Jesus? If He's too high up and no one can recognize Him, what's the point? He will have to be traveling at such an altitude that He is recognizable with the human eye. I don't have the answers to these questions, in fact, I have many more questions then answers. If He is traveling too fast and appears only as a blur streaking through the heavens, then again, what's the point?

Here's the issue that I want you to consider. This Second Coming Procession may take a great deal more time than we have ever imagined. Every eye must see Him (Rev.1:7) and I would add, see Him clearly. I can't for a second imagine that one of the most anticipated events in the history of mankind would end up being a rushed event. Jesus has been waiting for 2,000 years in eager anticipation of this moment and I seriously doubt that this will be a hurried affair. His Second Coming Procession will certainly take hours, possibly days and perhaps even take weeks. It definitely will not be measured in seconds or minutes.

However you view this event, please understand this: nothing in the history of mankind has ever come close or will ever surpass this event in its glory or its stunning impact on the inhabitants of the earth. This will be one glorious procession.

CHAPTER 16

The Procession Makes Landfall

While I am stretching your thinking, there are some other things I would ask you to consider. Remember, the entire Body of Christ is looking at the last days through very dark and obscure glasses (1 Cor.13:12). Although much of the prophetic end time revelation has been sealed until the end (Dan.12:4, 9) and seems securely under lock and key at the moment, I believe the Lord is greatly pleased with those who take the time to search out these matters. He commended the Bereans for their earnest pursuit of truth by diligently studying the Word of God (Acts 17:11). There are over a hundred chapters of scripture that deal in great detail with the last days and many things contained in them are still quite challenging. Proverbs 25:2 notes that, *"It is the glory of God to conceal a matter, but the glory of kings is to search out a matter."* It's like the Lord has us on this glorious treasure hunt (Prov.2:4) and He is encouraging us to go for it. He truly wants us to search these things out. He is delighted when we get in small groups and discuss these matters. He seems to be prodding us to begin a journey of discovery. He always reveals Himself to the hungry seeker.

What Goes Up … Must Come Down!

Again, most of us have thought of His appearing as an event that takes place so rapidly that if you were to bend over to tie your shoe - you might miss it. Like a fireworks display. They send up a rocket and it explodes, shooting brilliantly colored particles racing through the night sky.

Then suddenly, the beautiful colors fade and it's dark again. I assure you, His appearing will be vastly different than we have imagined.

There is another event that occurs soon after His Second Coming Procession is completed. This one actually takes place on the earth. The procession in the sky turns into a procession on the ground. The reason most of us have never heard of this before is because after His appearing, the credits started rolling and we exited the theater. We didn't realize that we had only made it to the first intermission and there was much more to come. We thought the intermission was the end of the show and so we walked out of the theater and missed some of the most stunning parts of the entire production. It's as though we sat through the previews and then left before the feature presentation began. Sounds odd but this is very similar to what has happened in the Body of Christ. We've been in such a rush to get raptured and leave the planet that we have never taken the time to discover His purpose for going through all the trouble. Does that make sense?

If it were possible to measure, on a hospital monitoring screen, the church's current understanding of events following the rapture, I believe it would be enlightening. The vital signs would immediately disappear and a loud beeper would sound, confirming that the patient had quickly expired. My point is that this is not a subject most of us have much knowledge about, nor have we given it serious consideration.

Let me introduce an entirely new paradigm of what is happening after His procession in the sky concludes. The part of this I haven't totally worked out yet is the sequence of events. In other words, I am very confident of the events themselves but it is difficult for me to place them in sequential order. The Bible doesn't offer a lot of clarity on the ordering of these events.

Quick End Time Overview

Let me digress for a moment. I am afraid I might confuse you if I just launch into this next section without a brief review. Jesus' Second Coming Procession is strategic in nature. There is much more going on here than His returning to blow minds and show off His glorified Bride (the church – Rev.19:7). He's returning to go to war against reprobate humans who hate God with a passion. They have become unredeemable and must be punished. After all, this is high treason and the end of the age time-clock is about to run out.

When Jesus returns, the earth will be in total disorder. The Antichrist has struggled to keep the world under his totalitarian rule. Shortly before the Lord's appearing, the Antichrist will experience a wave of resistance from several countries who find his leadership despicable (Dan.11:40-44). This break-down was prophesied in a dream given to Nebuchadnezzar and interpreted by Daniel (Dan.2:40-43). Things have started to unravel for the Antichrist. He has been busy slaughtering Christians and Jews by the millions (Dan.7:21; Rev.12:17). His campaign to conquer Jerusalem has been bogged down by massive supernatural disruptions. These setbacks came in the form of judgments and calamities. They were released by the two Witnesses, an empowered church and angelic decrees. This will be God's final attempt to turn man's heart back to Himself.

Note to the reader: We are at the point where immediately after the Abomination of Desolation the Antichrist is going about attempting to subdue the numerous pockets of resistance. His primary concern is the utter annihilation of every Jewish person as well as every Believer. Anyone who has any spiritual connection with God through His covenants must be eliminated. Before Jesus appears and raptures His church at the seventh trumpet, there have been a series of judgments that have devastated the planet. These judgments have been released by: (1) an empowered church (2) the two Witnesses and (3) by angels operating under God's direction. So far, thirteen of the scheduled twenty-one numbered judgments have been released by divine decree. The fourteenth is the seventh trumpet, at which time the church will be removed. I hope this review is helpful.

The Antichrist's Battle for Jerusalem

Although the Antichrist has faced many obstacles in trying to maintain a unified front, he has managed to convince most, if not all the nations, that it is imperative the Jews be purged from the earth.

One thing that is essential to understand is that God's end time drama all centers on Jerusalem. Although there has been a series of battles to capture Jerusalem, the Antichrist forces have been met with strong Jewish resistance.

> *And it shall come to pass **in all the land**, says the LORD, that **two-thirds** in it shall be **cut off and die**, but **one-third** shall be left in*

it: *(9)* **I will bring the one-third through the fire**
(Zech. 13:8-9)

This verse describes what many call, *"The Armageddon Campaign."* For the greater part of three-and-a-half years the Antichrist has been using the Valley of Megiddo as a staging area from which to mount his military strikes against the Jewish people. Armageddon is a geographic area located in the Valley of Megiddo. Shortly before the Lord returns, the Antichrist will have successfully wiped out over two-thirds of the Jewish population in the land of Israel. This is a greater massacre than the genocide that occurred in Nazi Germany.

For I will gather all the nations to battle against Jerusalem; the city shall be taken, the houses rifled, and the women ravished. Half of the city shall go into captivity, but the remnant of the people shall not be cut off from the city
(Zech.14:2)

I will also gather all nations, and bring them down to the Valley of Jehoshaphat [area of Jerusalem]; and I will enter into judgment with them there (12) "Let the nations be wakened, and come up to the Valley of Jehoshaphat; for there I will sit to judge all the surrounding nations. (14) Multitudes, multitudes in the valley of decision! For the day of the LORD is near in the valley of decision. (16) The LORD also will roar from

207

> *Zion [Jerusalem], and utter His voice from*
> *Jerusalem*
> *(Joel 3:2, 12, 14, and 16)*

Immediately prior to Jesus' return the Antichrist will have assembled a massive force to subdue and kill every Jewish person in the capitol city of Israel, Jerusalem. This will be a terrible time for the Jews as all nations align themselves against them. Many Jews will have been taken as slaves and put into forced labor camps in nearby nations (Ps.102:20).

This is a similar scenario to the one their Jewish ancestors faced when Pharaoh had them pressed up against the Red Sea. He thought there was nowhere for the Jews to escape. The same kind of scenario will happen again, however, this time the Jews will be trapped in the decimated city of Jerusalem. They will know their days are numbered as they will be surrounded and have absolutely no hope of escape.

This is the context into which the Second Coming Procession is placed. Without understanding this backdrop, what is getting ready to happen will be extremely difficult to process.

The Warrior King Returns

Jesus, the Warrior King, has returned to earth to receive from His Father the reward of His suffering. His Jewish brothers and sisters are fighting for their lives in Jerusalem. The Antichrist has killed two-thirds of the entire population of Israel. Many Jews are in prison camps; most appear to be in nearby countries. [Notes: The primary nations mentioned are Egypt and Assyria (Iraq). The

captives are called the "outcasts," the "dispersed ones," or
the "prisoners," (Isa.11:11-16; 27:13; Ps.102:20; Ps.147:2;
Hos.11:10-11; Zech.10:10)]

*Behold, the day of the LORD is coming
[Second Coming Procession] ... (2) for I will
gather [God is initiating this fight] <u>all the
nations</u> to battle against Jerusalem; the city
shall be taken, the houses rifled, and the
women ravished. Half of the city shall go
into captivity [Antichrist captures half of
Jerusalem], but the remnant of the people
shall not be cut off from the city. (3) Then the
LORD will go forth and fight against those
nations, as He fights in the day of battle. (4)
And in that day His feet will stand on the
Mount of Olives [Returns just as promised –
Acts 1] which faces Jerusalem on the east
and the Mount of Olives shall be split in two,
from east to west, making a very large
valley; half of the mountain shall move
toward the north And half of it toward the
south. (5) Then you shall flee through My
mountain valley [Jesus makes a way of
escape for the Jerusalem freedom fighters]
... Thus the LORD my God will come, and all
the saints with You. [This is Jesus and His
Second Coming Procession] (6) It shall come
to pass in that day that there will be no light;
the lights will diminish. [His return causes
massive cosmic disturbances] (7) It shall be
one day which is known to the LORD --*

209

*neither day nor night. But at evening time it
shall happen that it will be light
(Zech. 14:1-7)*

When Jesus ascended to heaven, after spending forty days teaching His disciples about the kingdom of heaven, the angels that accompanied Him promised that Jesus would return just as He departed (Acts 1:9-11). Taking a literal view of that promise, we could expect Him to return: (1) physically (2) geographically (3) visibly and (4) unmistakably. According to this passage in Zechariah 14, that is exactly how He intends to initiate His return. However, a few minor details have been left out, such as, when He returns He'll be bringing over a billion saints and angels with Him as well.

He has come for His Jewish people and to help them in their hour of greatest need. He has also returned to wipe out the Antichrist's armies as well as all the nations that have gathered from all over the earth. It's hard to determine if every single nation will be present, as there are currently about two hundred and ten different nations, but there will certainly be a strong showing. It is extremely likely that the United States will be among them, which is really unfortunate. I bring that up because verse 2, of our text above, uses the qualifier *"all nations."*

A Look Behind The Scenes

The Book of Joel (3:2-3) gives us three specific reasons why God has gathered this massive army in the land of Israel. They are: (1) they have scattered the Jewish people throughout the nations (2) they have been shamefully mistreated by those nations and (3) they have divided up the land God has specifically given to the Jewish people and given portions to others. If you know anything at all about the history of the Jewish people then you are aware of the accuracy of these statements. The primary reason for the greatest and final world war will center on the mistreatment of the Jewish people. This should raise a huge flag in our spirits and give intercessors a clear target.

One of the most descriptive accounts of what is happening here is recorded in graphic detail in Psalm 2.

Why do the nations rage, and the people plot a vain thing? (2) The kings of the earth set themselves [note the deliberate setting of their hearts and resources against Jesus], and the rulers take counsel together, against the LORD [the Father] and against His Anointed [Jesus], saying, (3) Let us break Their bonds in pieces [their desire is to cast away all godly constraint] And cast away Their cords from us. (4) He who sits in the heavens shall laugh; the LORD shall hold them in derision. (5) Then He shall speak to them in His wrath, and distress them in His deep displeasure: (6) Yet I have set My King on My holy hill of Zion [Jerusalem]. (7) I will declare the decree: the LORD has said to Me,' You are My Son, today I have begotten You. (8) Ask of Me, and I will give You the nations for Your inheritance, and the ends of the earth for Your possession. (9) You shall break them with a rod of iron; You shall dash them to pieces like a potter's vessel
   (Ps.2:1-9)

Why Jesus?

One of the strong confirmations that we are living in the last days is the growing number of people with an independent spirit that refuse to yield to man or God. These individuals have completely set themselves against God's authority and are desperately committed to having their own way. When Jesus returns with His saints and angelic host, this world will be getting ready to experience sweeping reforms. He will quickly deal with the nations who have gathered.

The really bizarre thing about this gathering of armies will be whom they have gathered to fight. They will not gather to fight one another, nor will they assemble to fight primarily against the Jews. They will have assembled to fight against and destroy Jesus and His army. Take this seriously. If you are a Believer, that means you will be part of this historic battle. If you are not a Believer, what are you waiting for? This would be an awesome time to surrender your heart to the glorious King, Jesus.

> *These will **make war with the Lamb**, and the Lamb will overcome them (Rev.17:14)*

> *And I saw the beast, the kings of the earth, and their armies, gathered together to **make***

> ***war against Him** who sat on the horse [Jesus] and against His army [saints and angels] (Rev.19:19)*

This group has plainly gathered for one purpose and that is to defeat Jesus and the host He has brought with Him in His Second Coming Procession. But here's the question of the hour. Why? Why are they coming to fight Jesus? What is it about Him that has them so upset?

Let me offer my best guess. I have spent a lot of time meditating on this event as it has captured my imagination. The reason for my intrigue is that it baffles me as to why anyone would even attempt something so foolish. There is certainly a reason why this information was written down and preserved for our consideration. God wants us to search out these matters. Let's take a look.

> *Woe to those who call evil good, and good evil; Who put darkness for light, and light for darkness; Who put bitter for sweet, and sweet for bitter!*
> *(Isa.5:20)*

One of the strong warnings that is consistently given to those living in the last days is to guard themselves against deception (Lk.21:8). The Bible says that many in the last days will refuse God's salvation and will choose to believe lies. Because of their stubborn refusal, they will be sent a strong delusion and they will apparently embrace this delusion rather than believe the truth. Whatever this delusion turns out to be, it is clearly connected with the Antichrist and his demonic leadership (2 Thess.2:11). I have a strong feeling it will have to do with the following passage of scripture.

> *He [the Antichrist] shall speak pompous words against the Most High, shall persecute*

> *the saints of the Most High, and* **shall intend**
> **to change times and law**
> *(Dan.7:25)*

These are three immense statements. The first two are easily understood and the third is a bit more troublesome. The Antichrist will: (1) blaspheme God (2) kill His saints and (3) attempt to change times and law.

How does one attempt to change *"times and law"*? I would guess that means that part of the Antichrist's agenda involves modifying calendars and amending laws. The calendar adjustments make sense since everything currently revolves around the birth of Christ (BC–AD). That's certainly one thing he wants hidden from public view.

What about the laws he wants to change? Why change laws? The primary purpose of establishing laws is to govern or control human behavior. God gave His law at Mt. Sinai to govern the conduct of His people. Laws decide whether a society will be moral or immoral. Laws determine what a particular people value. Laws therefore lay a foundation upon which a society determines it's moral, ethical, legal and spiritual course. Whoever establishes the laws will also control the people over which those laws apply. Does that make sense? This is why the Antichrist purposes to set up an entirely new system of law. Unfortunately, the Bible is unclear as to how successful he is in this effort as we are only told that he *"shall intend to change times and law."* We are left with an unanswered question as to whether he will be victorious or not. My hunch, unfortunately, is that he will be extremely successful.

A Second Look

Let's revisit our original question that brought us to this point. Why have all these nations gathered to fight against Jesus? What has He done to incur such vile indignation?

I am convinced that the events we have mentioned are all tied together. Men will exercise their free will and turn against God. The law of iniquity is stronger than most of us realize and will be clearly exposed at the conclusion of Jesus' Millennial reign. Once men choose to disregard God's ways and God's laws, they will be offered a *"strong delusion"* in its place. God's laws will quickly be exchanged for the Antichrist's laws. Why? Because he is lawlessness personified. So what kind of laws might he establish? This isn't too tough to figure out because we understand the nature of the spirit that is behind the Antichrist, which is Satan himself. He will allow the kind of laws that reflect his demonic nature. He will enact laws that destroy, kill and rob (Jn.10:10) people of their humanity. He is well aware that we were created in the very image of God, and he will do everything in his power to corrupt our fallen humanity by permitting us to engage in practices that violate God's laws and thereby cause mankind to go into a self-destruct mode. This is why Jesus said, *"Unless those days were shortened no flesh would survive"* (Matt.24:22). He has a firm grasp of the enemy's plans and is fully cognizant of where this is all heading.

Once Satan's foothold is established through the removal of laws that encourage and even reward immoral conduct, it's like the last day chess game has suddenly moved into checkmate. Humanity is now on a fast track to obliteration. All resistance is being slowly and methodically

215

eliminated. God's character is being ruthlessly assaulted on a daily basis by the Antichrist. The church is being systematically dismantled and removed through martyrdom. And in addition to all this, laws that allow mankind to violate and undermine their very existence are being enacted and even hailed as progressive. Once this occurs, the human race will have chosen a course of action that can only be salvaged by the speedy return of Jesus Christ.

The Reprobates

By this time, those who have managed to survive God's judgments will be fully-committed God-haters. The Antichrist will have them totally convinced that he is God and that Jesus Christ is nothing more than an extremely ambitious spiritual imposter. The Antichrist will also persuade them that Jesus is a huge threat and must be eliminated. They will see and understand Jesus to be as evil and depraved as Christians believe the Antichrist to be. Do you see how warped and twisted things have become? Evil is now considered totally good and good evil. This is how the reprobate mind processes things. So many signs and wonders will have been happening during the last three-and-a-half years that most people won't know what to make of all this. They will be convinced that Jesus is totally evil and is coming to make them submit to His control. They will perceive Jesus to be an enormous threat and will believe that He must be eliminated at all costs. They will be in full agreement with the Antichrist and will do everything in their power to see God destroyed.

And in that day His feet will stand on the Mount of Olives [Returns just as promised – Acts 1] which faces Jerusalem on the east and the Mount of Olives shall be split in two, from east to west, making a very large valley; half of the mountain shall move toward the north And half of it toward the south. (5) Then you shall flee through My mountain valley [Jesus makes a way of escape for the Jerusalem freedom fighters] ... Thus the LORD my God will come, and all the saints with You (Zech.14:4-5)

These are fascinating verses of scripture. Jesus returns to the exact spot from which He ascended 2,000 years earlier and in direct fulfillment of the prophetic word. The Jewish freedom fighters that have been trapped in Jerusalem are desperately out-numbered and barely hanging on. Two-thirds of all the Jews living in Israel have been executed and the third still alive is about to be crushed by the Antichrist's coalition of armies supplied by the union of nations across the earth.

Jehovah-nic-a-time!

Just as Moses and the children of Israel, when backed up to the Red Sea, experienced a miraculous deliverance, in the same dramatic fashion, Jesus will return. It will be at the precise moment of the Jewish freedom fighters pending demise that He will supernaturally deliver His people once again. One of my names for God is

"Jehovah-nic-a-time". He just instinctively knows exactly when to show up in our lives.

Jesus does for this Jewish fighting force the same thing He did for Moses. However, instead of parting a sea, He gets creative and parts a mountain. The Jewish soldiers take advantage of their good fortune and run for their lives through the valley created when the Mount of Olives splits. Just as the children of Israel escaped to safety through the Red Sea, these Israelis will escape to safety through the mountain.

> *But, beloved, do not forget this one thing, that with the Lord one day is as a thousand years, and a thousand years as one day. (9) The Lord is not slack concerning His promise, as some count slackness, but is longsuffering toward us, not willing that any should perish but that all should come to repentance*
> *(2 Pet.3:8-9).*

CHAPTER 17

Introduction to the Millennial Kingdom

If you ask average Believers what is going to take place when they die you will generally hear something like, "Go to heaven and be with Jesus." Certainly in the broadest and most general sense that is true but in terms of specifics that tiny scrap of information is not overly helpful. If you follow that response with, "Okay, anything else?" they might respond with, "I think I'll walk on streets of gold and maybe sit on a cloud and play a harp or something." Now they have exhausted their entire knowledge banks and most of that information contains only fragments of biblical reality.

Information about the Millennial Kingdom is probably the most misunderstood and therefore the most neglected subject in today's western church. This is both tragic as well as dangerous. I say that because this happens to be the very information that was written by God to instruct and prepare His end time church for the coming global firestorm, as well as the glorious kingdom age that will follow.

I believe you will find the following information to be fascinating. I also believe it will assist you in connecting the dots in terms of your destiny as a Believer. You will see and discover realms of glory you probably never thought or imagined were available. What you will realize is that there is a much bigger purpose for your life as a Believer than you ever imagined. So prepare your heart to step into a whole new level of destiny.

> *... having made known to us the mystery [something hidden that He intends to make plain] of His will, according to His good pleasure which He purposed in Himself, (10) that in the dispensation of the fullness of the times He might gather together in one all things in Christ, both which are in heaven and which are on earth -- in Him. (11) In Him also we have obtained an inheritance* (Eph.1:9-11)

The centerpiece of God's eternal purpose is for Jesus to come back and fully establish His kingdom rule over the earth. He will do this by joining together the natural and the spiritual realm. Through His creative genius the Son of God will join these two dimensions together to express God's true personality and kingdom purposes. Please note that the Apostle Paul adds that not only will God merge the spiritual realm with the physical realm, but also, into that very setting, the church will receive her inheritance and discover her true identity.

Since childhood I was taught to pray, *"Let Your kingdom come and Your will be done on earth as it is in heaven"* (Matt 6:10). I thought I was just asking God to allow good things to happen on earth similar to the good things that are taking place in heaven. There certainly is truth in that line of thinking but there is also much more understanding to be gained from that simple prayer as well.

What no one ever told me was that the ultimate expression of this prayer was clearly stated in the words that Jesus instructed His disciples to pray. He wanted His church crying out for the future establishment of the kingdom of God to take place on this earth.

An entirely new paradigm for most Believers is that we are not going to heaven; heaven is coming to earth. Christians, who have gone to be with the Lord from the cross to the present, go to heaven with a disembodied spirit. Why is that? In heaven a body is unnecessary. It is a spiritual realm and only requires our spirit to be present. We can fully participate in the heavenly realm without the use of physical assistance. In fact, our physical bodies would be extremely cumbersome and serve more of a hindrance than a help in that environment.

We are currently living in the partial, waiting for the substantial, in order to experience the ultimate. What does that mean? The partial is our limited participation and experience in relationship to His kingdom. George Ladd calls this, *"The already, but not yet."* Everything about our current kingdom experience is partial. Because of the limitations of our physical bodies and having to live in a fallen environment, our ability to enjoy and participate in His kingdom is greatly handicapped.

When Jesus returns and establishes His kingdom on this earth, every aspect of our lives will instantly experience a substantial increase. We will be immediately transformed in both our bodies and our spirits.

> *Do not remember the former things, [negative circumstances of this present age] nor consider the things of old. (19) Behold, I will do a new thing, now it shall spring forth; shall you not know it?*
> *(Isa.43:18-19)*

> *But as it is written, Eye hath not seen, nor ear heard, neither have entered into the*

> *heart of man, the things which God hath*
> *prepared for them that love him*
> *(1 Cor.2:9)*

The Millennial Kingdom is both awesome and full of wonder and discovery. The Prophet Isaiah declares that when God releases His Son's glorious kingdom, it will surpass expectation and confound our current intellectual capacity. In other words, it's better than what we have heard or thought and it's larger in scope than our current limitations will permit us to comprehend.

Those who mistakenly teach that the fullness of Jesus' kingdom is already here on earth make those kinds of statements because they are uninformed about the coming reality of His Millennial Kingdom. Most of the Body of Christ falls into that category which is why I felt compelled to write this book. For many of us, this is an entirely new subject.

Why is it important for Believers to know about the Millennial Kingdom? How can an event so far in the future have any relevance in our life today? These are important questions and deserve clear answers. Let me list a few reasons that I think you will find helpful.

First of all, having understanding of the Millennial Kingdom will help establish your heart in the truth of Jesus' ultimate victory over every adversary and situation that includes Satan and all forms of darkness (1 Cor.15:57-58). Secondly, it will allow you to understand the dynamic continuity that exists between this life and the coming age. This is a huge subject that we will cover later. I think you will be amazed at what we discover. Thirdly, there are over a hundred chapters of Bible that deal with end time matters. Therefore, ignorance of these subjects greatly limits our ability to discern God's last day purposes. It would be like setting out to sea and having no maps to help you navigate. That would be both unwise and completely impractical. Lastly, understanding the Millennial Kingdom will expand your understanding of the beauty of Jesus and that revelation will translate into greater passion and purity.

Let's begin our journey by looking at some key passages of scripture that I think will be extremely helpful.

> *And I saw an angel come down from heaven, having the key of the bottomless pit and a great chain in his hand. (2) And he laid hold on the dragon, that old serpent, which is the Devil, and Satan, and bound him a thousand years, (3) And cast him into the bottomless pit, and shut him up, and set a seal upon him, that he should deceive the nations no more, till the thousand years should be fulfilled: and after that he must be loosed a little season*
> *(Rev.20:1-3)*

A few verses prior to these in Revelation 19 we are told that when Jesus returns to earth to devour His enemies, after slaying the armies that have gathered to make war with Him, He immediately begins dealing with the unholy trinity. The Antichrist and the False Prophet are the first to be disposed of by being thrown into the Lake of Fire. These are the first to experience this horrific torment and will do so alone until the end of Jesus' Millennial Reign. At that time, the unsaved will stand before God to be judged. The thing I want you to see is that the first order of business on Jesus busy agenda is to deal with Satan, his puppet ruler the

Antichrist and his spiritual advisor the False Prophet. This dynamic diabolical trio are now totally subdued.

With the Antichrist and False Prophet confined forever to the Lake of Fire, commonly referred to as *"hell"*, Jesus now turns His fury on the Dragon (Satan). Please notice how quickly and effortlessly Satan is rendered useless. Also take note to whom God assigns the task of dealing with the Devil. Jesus simply sends *"a no name angel"* to take care of business. For all of those who were expecting Jesus to bring in His heavy lifting crew, Michael and Gabriel, the Lord apparently doesn't even allow them to dirty their hands. They are completely unnecessary.

Whoever this angel is, he has absolutely no fear of Satan whatsoever. If you read in between the lines, it even appears that this angel manhandles Satan. Not only is there no sign of intimidation, when I read this account, I come away with the distinct feeling that Satan is shocked and bewildered. He apparently is taken into custody so quickly that he appears to offer no resistance at all. I think he's stunned, bewildered and totally perplexed that this is really happening. He has lived in denial for so long, that when confronted with reality, he is completely unequipped to deal with his circumstance.

The angel wastes no time in binding the Devil and placing him in solitary confinement in his temporary holding cell, which the Bible calls *"The bottomless pit."* Although no other explanation is provided, the very term *"bottomless pit,"* gives us a pretty clear description that lets us know that this is not the country-club type of confinement. This is hard-core and he will not enjoy his stay for a moment. Verses two and three tell us that Satan is bound-up, shut-up and sealed-up. You get the distinct feeling that his confinement has been well thought through and nothing further needs to be done to secure him.

Please notice the length of his incarceration in *"The bottomless pit"* is 1,000 years. This is repeated no less than six times in this brief chapter. We are told that at the end of this 1,000-year season of confinement that he will be let out on parole for a very brief and unspecified period of time.

> *And I saw thrones, and they sat upon them, and judgment was given unto them: and I saw the souls of them that were beheaded for the witness of Jesus, and for the word of God, and which had not worshipped the beast, neither his image, neither had received his mark upon their foreheads, or in their hands; and they lived and reigned with Christ a thousand years*
> *(Rev.20:4)*

There has been much discussion around trying to identify who these individuals are that are occupying these thrones and making judgments. Some say they are the twenty-four elders (Rev.5:10). Others say they are the twelve Apostles (Lk.22:28-30). Still others speculate these are the ones who were beheaded for their faithful witness to Christ and His Word. I believe those sitting on the thrones and making judgments are the ones who have already received authorization to do so. The promise of sitting on the thrones was given to a general group called: (1) His Bride (Rev.19:7-9) (2) overcomers (Rev.2:26-27) (3) the church (1 Cor.6:2) (4) the armies of Christ (Rev.19:14) and (5) His servants (Rev.22:3-5).

Those who fight in battles always participate in dividing up the spoils. They are the ones who assume the rulership over the conquered entity. In this case they are the saints of the Most High who have returned with Jesus and have been given authority to rule and reign with Him (Rev.5:10; 22:3-5).

> *But the rest of the dead lived not again until the thousand years were finished. This is the first resurrection. (6) Blessed and holy is he that hath part in the first resurrection: on such the second death hath no power, but they shall be priests of God and of Christ, and shall reign with him a thousand years (Rev.20:5-6)*

Those described as *"The rest of the dead"* are unbelievers. They do not have the privilege of participating in the *"first resurrection"* but will be raised up during the *"second resurrection"* and will take part in the *"second death"* which consists of everlasting confinement in the *"lake of fire"*. These unbelievers will be brought back to life and face God's bar of justice after the 1,000 year Millennial Reign of Christ.

Both Old Testament and New Testament Believers will be raised during the *"first resurrection"* and will rule and reign with Christ forever (22:3-5). The statement, *"On such the second death hath no power,"* serves as final confirmation of their favored status and privilege of ruling and reigning with Christ for all eternity. If in the back of your mind you are still thinking *"harps and clouds"* you are still totally missing the point. The future destiny of His people is so awesome that words are completely inadequate to express or describe such glory.

The rest of Revelation 20 deals with the very end of Christ's 1,000-year reign on the earth and then follows that with the unbelievers' judgment that takes place immediately after the Millennium. There is a massive amount of biblical information that is sandwiched in between the beginning of the Millennial Reign of Christ and Satan's futile rebellion at the very end of the Millennium. This is where you and I are headed and why these things are so exciting to study. This is not *"pie in the sky"* Christianity. Rather, this is a living reality and will one day be known and taught as Christianity 101.

CHAPTER 18

Life in the Millennial Kingdom

Repent ... so that times of refreshing may come from the presence of the Lord, (20) and that He may send Jesus Christ, ... (21) whom heaven must receive [Jesus must remain in heaven until certain things transpire on the earth] until the times of restoration of all things, which God has spoken by the mouth of all His holy prophets since the world began
(Acts 3:19-21)

Jesus is currently being retained in heaven until a series of events described by the prophets have been completed. There is a statement that we have all heard numerous times by various teachers. They say that, "Jesus could return at any moment to gather His people." Although this may sound promising and even comforting, in reality, it is a very misleading statement. For those of you who have made it this far, I hope you understand that there are many significant events that the Word of God has declared must transpire before Jesus will be authorized by His Father to return to earth. It is important that we have a biblical understanding of these things so we are not tossed about and led into confusion by every new idea that seems to emerge. As the time of His appearing approaches, there will be a flood of different perspectives on the last days. If you stay humble and teachable, the Holy Spirit will continue to lead you into all truth. You have absolutely nothing to fear. His sheep still hear His voice (Jn.10:4) and He will keep and protect us from the deception that is coming upon the whole earth.

Restoration of All Things

When Jesus returns, the period known as the *"Restoration of all things"* begins. This will be a glorious time. Just being in the manifest presence of Jesus will be a delight that is indescribable.

This will be a period of great recovery and change. It will also probably be much different than many have assumed. Remember, the earth has been experiencing twenty-one horrific judgments that have left marks on every square foot of the earth's surface. Nothing has escaped unaffected. The planet that once hosted the Garden of Eden has now been totally ravished by three-and-a-half-years of violence, bloodshed, plagues, pestilence, earthquakes, sea-life destruction, plant-life incineration, removal of mountains, solar disruption, poisoned water supplies and depleted food resources.

At the beginning of the Millennial reign of Jesus, Satan is imprisoned (20:2) and his two associates *The Antichrist* and *The False Prophet* are spending their days in the *Lake of Fire* (19:20). Although we are not told in the Book of Revelation what happens to Satan's demonic forces, we know they are assigned a place in the *Lake of Fire*: "*Then He will also say to those on the left hand, depart from Me, you cursed, into the everlasting fire prepared for the devil and his angels*" (Matt 25:41). We can assume they are either imprisoned with the devil in the *Bottomless Pit* and will be freed with him near the end of the Millennial Kingdom or they have joined *The Antichrist* and *The False Prophet* in the *Lake of Fire*. Either way they will not escape being punished (Isa.24:21). We are only told that Satan will be released near the end of the 1,000 years, so it is possible that he is doing his deceptive work solo. If the demons are assigned to the *Lake of Fire* along with *The Antichrist* and *The False Prophet*, then they will not be working with Satan at that time. How can we be sure of that? Because the *Lake of Fire* is a permanent abode. Unlike Satan's temporary holding tank, *the Bottomless Pit*, once someone is thrown into the *Lake of Fire*, they do not come out, ever (Rev.20:10). It is a place that has been prepared, by God, to host the devil, his fallen angels and unbelievers for all eternity.

The point I am making is that the earth is in total disarray, and all forms of darkness and evil influences are now totally removed and offer absolutely no possibility of negative interference. The earth and all that has survived has finally been liberated by the mighty King of Kings and Lord of Lords.

The Great Tribulation Aftermath

The picture I want you to put in your mind is the footage we have all seen countless times of the aftermath of World War II. Most cities have been utterly destroyed and many are nothing more than smoldering ruins. The smell of rotting flesh is disgusting and is everywhere. There are literally billions of dead bodies of men and animals scattered throughout the earth in various stages of decay and are being consumed by the fowls of the air (19:21b).

As we stand and survey the landscape, the carnage and utter devastation appear more like something out of some science fiction movie with graphic special effects then it does real life. This is horrible. The only good news is that Jesus is among us and His enemies are no longer a threat. But where does one start to repair such extensive damage?

Most people who have given this any thought figure that Jesus will gather all His saints together, wave His hands and say, *"Earth be healed,"* and magically all the smoke, dead bodies and negative circumstances are no longer an issue. Where once stood smoldering ruins, now stand beautiful buildings, clean and newly constructed homes, located in spotless neighborhoods, complete with new playgrounds and immaculate parks.

That might make a great movie but I think it will be far from the reality we will discover when the initial stages of recovery are implemented. Please keep in mind that the Millennial Kingdom will be a time when God joins together the heavenly realm with the material and physical realm. That means that things are neither all supernatural nor are they entirely physical. It will be a brilliant merging together of both of these realms (Eph.1:9-10). This has been in the heart of God from the very beginning. The awesome thing is that Jesus is in full control and has a well-designed and thought through plan. He knows exactly what needs to be done and His magnificent leadership will get the massive job of recovery started immediately. It will also be accomplished in the most efficient manner possible with crews of people working in total unity and with joyful spirits.

Excuse Me ... Did Someone Say Work?

I know I just lost a few of you with the word "work". You thought you would be issued a harp and assigned a cloud while Jesus did all the work. Sorry to disappoint you but things will probably be radically different than you might have anticipated. There is no telling how long the reconstruction will take but the task at hand is immense. Again, I want you to picture the aftermath of World War II. Superimpose that picture over the entire earth and imagine what it will take to bury the dead, remove the rubble and rebuild cities in order to make them fit for human occupation. This is a task suited for only one man and His name is Jesus.

The war in Iraq has given the people of the United States a realistic view of the daunting task involved in restoring a nation that has been ravished by war and civil unrest. Few anticipated the enormous challenge we would face once Saddam Hussein's brutal regime was removed from power.

Now imagine that scenario played over the 210 nations of the earth that have experienced an infinitely greater devastation than Iraq. Try to visualize what it will take in manpower and in human ingenuity to approach such a monumental task. Where do you start? How do you set priorities on such a mammoth project?

I could write an entire book on the challenges of such a rebuilding effort. But here's the really fantastic news. Jesus not only has a plan, but He will dazzle us with the wisdom and creative approaches He introduces. Remember, darkness is bound in a *Bottomless Pit* and there are no sinful influences to distract or to hinder. This will be more helpful than most of us can imagine. Also remember that Jesus and His Father, assisted by the Holy Spirit, have been planning all this since before the foundations of the world (Eph.1:9-10). They are not surprised by sin's destructive power and are fully up to the task of global restoration. Their plans are full of wisdom and will cause everyone to marvel and erupt into spontaneous worship as their plans begin to emerge.

Moses and the Millennial Kingdom

God's plans to join together natural processes with supernatural resources will be one of the great surprises in the age to come. Remember, Moses was given two tablets that were carved out of stone and written by the supernatural finger of God (Ex.32:16). After the originals were broken due to the sin of God's people, Moses was assigned the task of carving the second set (Ex.34:1). God added His supernatural touch and once again inscribed His law on the tablets provided by Moses. God provided all the material and did all the labor the first time around, however, after His people sinned, man got involved in the process of restoration. This is the same pattern that will emerge during the Millennial Kingdom when the greater Moses, Jesus, reigns over the earth. There will be a merging of both the natural and supernatural processes. They will be joined together in an incredibly creative and dynamic way, just as happened to Moses. Remember, as a result of his experience, Moses' face shone so brightly that he had to put a veil over it. Our faces will also become radiant when we experience the process of divine partnership at an entirely new level.

Another one of the things that has puzzled most researchers when it comes to the Millennial Kingdom is identifying who the saints are supposed to rule over during this time. If those who received the *"Mark of the beast"* are destined for the *Lake of Fire* (Rev.14:11) and if those who came up to do battle against Jesus when He returned have been executed, who else is alive for the saints to govern?

Most Bible commentators faced with this dilemma seem to cave under pressure. Here is their common answer. Most, by the way, approach the end times from a dispensational pre-millennial point of view. That simply means they believe the rapture happens prior to the Tribulation Period. So with the church being removed prior to the Tribulation, those left behind miraculously start getting saved. This is really quite unusual as the Bible clearly favors the use of gospel preachers to accomplish this task (Rom.10:14-15). These individuals who are saved during the Tribulation Period and who make it through to the end without facing martyrdom, then go into the next age alive without a glorified body, but fully redeemed.

Although there are many things about this explanation that are perplexing, the most troubling to me is the status of these poor Tribulation saints. After having to suffer through the most horrific circumstances any generation of Believers has ever had to endure, their only reward is that they make the transition from one age to the next alive and still faithful. All their dead friends have been resurrected and have received glorified bodies but these poor souls have to persevere through the next age with old equipment and a serious case of *Post Traumatic Stress Disorder*. Doesn't seem quite like the way God operates nor does it square with His Word. The Bible is clear and promises those still alive when Jesus returns that they can expect to be caught-up to meet the Lord in the air and receive new bodies as well (1 Thess.4:15-18). None are ever mentioned to have been forgotten, neglected or left behind.

Who Are These Guys?

So, who are those who make the transition alive but in natural bodies? As with every other brutal dictatorship in human history, there has always been a group that resists and refuses to comply with a new regimes' policies and edicts. Even the most brutal dictators like Hitler and Stalin had huge numbers of non-compliant citizens. Most were not opposed for religious reasons but for reasons of conscience, politics and principle. There is absolutely no reason to believe that this trend will suddenly change because a world dictator shows up on the scene. Certainly, he will be convincing and extremely deceptive. However, even as cunning and deceptive as Adolf Hitler turned out to be, he had masses of defectors. He had those who were disenfranchised with his leadership and expressed serious concerns about his plans for world domination.

It stands to reason that the *Antichrist* will also experience huge numbers of resistors who will refuse *The Mark of the Beast* for a number of reasons. When considering the global population, this small percentage could easily number in the tens of millions. Threats of execution will not deter this group as they are free thinkers and are not inclined to cower under pressure. They will rather face execution than yield their individual rights to the Antichrist's collective society. The challenge of personal survival is much more appealing to them than surrendering to a system that seizes control through fear and intimidation. They will not be bullied and compromise is not an option. They will refuse the *Mark of the Beast* and will creatively find alternate ways to survive. Many will be beheaded for their stubborn refusal but that is more palatable to them than violating their principles of personal autonomy.

Although we have no way of knowing the exact number of these survivors, it will certainly be substantial. God will reward them for their courageous refusal to yield to the Antichrist's demands. These will be given access and by the grace of God, be allowed to participate in the establishing of His Son's Kingdom. These could be known as the resisters. The Bible simply refers to them as, *"Those who are left in all the nations"* (Zech.14:16).

Sinners in the Millennial Kingdom?

For many, the thought of sinners being allowed to enter the newly established kingdom is shocking and even offensive. How can we be sure that such a group will be permitted entrance into Jesus Millennial Kingdom? The first way we can be sure is by the unambiguous testimony from the Word of God itself.

> *No more shall an infant from there live but a few days, nor an old man who has not fulfilled his days; For the child shall die one hundred years old, but the SINNER being one hundred years old shall be accursed (Isa.65:20)*

This text is embedded in a Millennial Kingdom context and cannot be understood or interpreted any other way. This verse makes it clear that life expectancy will be greatly enhanced during Jesus' righteous rule. It appears that God will accomplish this by reversing the curse He declared in Genesis 3:16-19. Unsaved humans will live hundreds of years during the Millennial reign of Jesus. Crib deaths and infant childhood diseases will be unheard of and men and women will live out long lives that will last hundreds of years. Only those who willfully violate or rebel against Jesus' authority will die prematurely. Sin and rebellion will be dealt with swiftly and decisively (Rev.2:27).

> *And it shall come to pass that everyone who is left of all the nations which came against Jerusalem shall go up from year to year to worship the King, the LORD of hosts, and to keep the Feast of Tabernacles.* (17) *And it shall be that whichever of the families of the earth do not come up to Jerusalem to worship the King, the LORD of hosts, on them there will be no rain.* (18) *If the family of Egypt will not come up and enter in, they shall have no rain; they shall receive the plague with which the LORD strikes the nations who do not come up to keep the Feast of Tabernacles.* (19) *This shall be the punishment of Egypt and the punishment of all the nations that do not come up to keep the Feast of Tabernacles*
> *(Zech.14:16-19)*

This verse is a clear warning to those alive during the Millennial Kingdom who refuse to obey Jesus' command to celebrate the Feast of Tabernacles. The consequences for failing to comply will be understood by those living at that time and there will be no exceptions. Jesus' Word will be known throughout the kingdom and those who attempt to disregard it will be penalized. Rain is essential for raising crops and those who willfully violate his word will deeply regret it. Entire nations will come under judgment if they choose to ignore His commands. No nation will be exempt. The feasts of the Lord mentioned in Leviticus 23 will be celebrated with compliance being mandatory (Ez.45:21).

> *Now when the thousand years have expired, Satan will be released from his prison (8) and will go out to deceive the nations which are in the four corners of the earth, ... to gather them together to battle, whose number is as the sand of the sea. (9) They went up on the breadth of the earth and surrounded the camp of the saints and the beloved city*
> *(Rev. 20:7-9)*

If there were no unsaved people alive during Jesus' Kingdom Reign, Satan would be unsuccessful in his efforts to gather an army and this entire passage would make absolutely no sense. It is clear that he will amass a vast army that will come up against Jesus' *millennial headquarters* in Jerusalem. We will have more to say about this later. However, as you can see, the passages that deal with rebellious sinners during Jesus Millennial Kingdom are not ambiguous.

It goes without saying that if there is a group that is assigned the task of ruling and reigning, then there must be another group over whom they exercise that authority. It makes no sense that Believers would be exercising that dimension of power and control over other Believers. However, as is the case in all Christian organizations, there certainly will be an authority structure of some kind and there will be different levels of responsibility. Jesus' criteria for key leadership positions are faithfulness, meekness (how we served others), love and godly understanding (Lk.22:26).

CHAPTER 19

The Dynamic Convergence

Those in natural bodies will be given the important task of repopulating the earth. Resurrected saints living in glorified bodies will not be involved with reproduction (Mk.12:24-25).

One of the surprising activities that might seem odd to some, is the concept of rebuilding or the actual physical reconstruction (Isa.61:4) of the earth.

> *They shall build houses and inhabit them; they shall plant vineyards and eat their fruit (Isa.65:21).*

> *And My elect shall long enjoy the work of their hands. (23) They shall not labor in vain (Isa.65:22-23).*

> *And they shall rebuild the old ruins, they shall raise up the former desolations, and they shall repair the ruined cities (Isa.61:4).*

Some have either neglected or *"spiritualized"* these types of verses to the point that they miss the wealth of information they provide. There are literally hundreds of verses that supply us with valuable insight about the age to come. Neglecting these verses will prove foolish and even spiritually detrimental.

I have no idea as to who will be assigned to which specific tasks, but it is clear that manual labor will be involved in the process. Two reasons I want you to understand this is: (1) because the earth is going to be in a very desolate condition near the end of this age and will need great attention to make it habitable again and (2) I want us to have a realistic understanding of the processes that will be employed to make the earth usable to sustain life during the repopulation and reconstruction stage. Jesus will not simply show-up, sprinkle magic fairy dust and *"presto-bam-o"* you have a brand new earth with an instant Garden of Eden environment. The reconstruction stage will take work and diligence to complete. There will be an incredible spirit of cooperation, supernatural joy and vision for the task of restoration. The big difference will be Jesus' active participation and coaching. He will give us living understanding of how to approach different tasks. We will marvel at His kindness and patience. His gracious speech will never cease to astound us. His encouragement and appreciation for every single person will provide awesome motivation for the difficult work projects. There will be absolutely no partiality shown by Him. He will treat the one assigned to simple tasks with as much respect and esteem as those who have been given larger responsibilities. The parable of the talents will make more sense than we can imagine (Matt.25:20-23).

The Merging of the Natural and Spiritual Realms

I really want us to understand the key insight that the New Testament provides for gaining revelation of what is happening during the age to come. I will repeat this often for the sake of firmly establishing this truth in our spirits. The interpretative key to understanding the way things will be structured in the age to come is found in Ephesians 1:9-

10. Without understanding this mysterious passage, the Millennial Kingdom will continue to be an enigma. The Holy Spirit has offered us these verses to assist us and to bring hundreds of passages of scripture out of the shadows and into the light.

> *Having made known to us the mystery of His will, according to His good pleasure which He purposed in Himself, (10) that in the dispensation of the fullness of the times He might gather together in one all things in Christ, both which are in heaven and which are on earth -- in Him*
> *(Eph.1:9-10)*

When the Bible mentions the word *"mystery"* it always puts it in the context of discovery. A biblical mystery is something that has been hidden for a season and then revealed so that God's people will have the needed insight at precisely the right moment. I personally am persuaded that the Holy Spirit is releasing new insights concerning the age to come to help prepare His Bride for the brewing storm and to fascinate us through the process of discovery. He loves to dazzle and excite His people with new revelation. They are His fiery kisses to our cold hearts (Song of Sol.1:2).

Also notice that His secret passion has been to merge the spiritual realm (things in heaven) with the natural realm (things on earth). He will blend these with such extravagant wisdom and such comprehensive understanding that we will never cease to be awestruck with the things that come out of His mouth every time He speaks. The Millennial Kingdom will be full of supernatural activity (Jn.14:12) but it will be activated and processed through natural life circumstances. God is not intending to suspend natural processes for the sake of His supernatural processes. He will combine the two in stunning fashion.

Heavenly Bodies

Our glorified bodies will free us from the need to rest. Therefore, there will be no need for beds for His saints in the age to come. Our glorified body will have the same natural and supernatural qualities as Jesus' had. Our new body will be physical in nature. It can be touched because it has substance. It is not made of air, neither is it some kind of spooky mirage. It is real and tangible. However, like Jesus' glorified body, it has the ability to walk through walls and appear and disappear when necessary. It can be in one place one moment and in another location a moment later. It is not bound by time or space. It can eat real food but has no need or capacity for the elimination of substances it consumes. In that sense our bodies will be similar to the angels in heaven (Mk.12:25). It will look like us and we will be known and recognized by friends and family members. The vanity of personal appearance will be removed, as that was part of the curse and will not be an issue ever again. There will be no need of mirrors in God's new creation (Rev.21:5). We will have absolutely no regard for ourselves but will be passionately in love with God and His people. Fulfilling the greatest commandment will be our daily obsession (Mk.12:29-31).

Longevity of the Word of God

Another great surprise will be the desire and interest we will have for the Word of God. Most have assumed that either we will have instant understanding of the scriptures and therefore Bible study will be irrelevant, or that we will have obtained such a high degree of spiritual maturity that it will be unnecessary. Nothing could be further from the truth. In the age to come, His Word will be opened to us in a way that will delight and amaze us. We will be just like the four living creatures who never tire of beholding the one seated on the throne because they receive stunning fresh revelation every time they take another glance (Rev.4:8). We will marvel with endless fascination at the wisdom contained in His Word. Our hearts will be growing in revelation and in our understanding of the beauty of the Son of God throughout all eternity. We will never reach a plateau because our understanding will continue to go from one level of glory to the next.

> *But we all, with unveiled face, beholding as in a mirror the glory of the Lord, are being transformed into the same image from glory to glory , just as by the Spirit of the Lord (2 Cor.3:18)*

Many of us have mistakenly thought that when Jesus returns we will be instantly mature and suddenly know everything that God knows. This is grossly inaccurate. There will be new levels of discovery throughout all eternity. We will never tire of His insights nor will we become bored for even an instant. His Word will be more helpful and relevant in the next age than we

245

have ever imagined. We will grow in both our understanding and our appreciation of it throughout the endless ages. Peter hinted to this reality when he described God's Word as, *"The Word of God which lives and abides forever"* (1 Peter 1:23).

Like the children of Israel who received fresh manna every day, so will be the stunning new revelations we will be receiving consistently (Lam.3:23). These will be daily tokens of His faithful love and we will understand them as, *"The firstfruits of His increase"* (Jer.2:3).

> *Of the increase of His government and peace*
> *there will be no end*
> *(Isa.9:7)*

Increase is a kingdom standard. By that I mean that in every dimension of life, whether it relates to task orientation, relational matters or spiritual concepts, we will forever be growing. We will experience significant increase in our depth of admiration for the kindness and brilliance of the Son of God. We will never become exhausted with His Word, as it will be continually unfolded in our hearts with living understanding of its contents. No one falls asleep in Jesus' Bible studies.

Enjoyable Prayer

The same is true of prayer. Prayer will be one of the most joyful activities which will engage our hearts during the Millennial Kingdom (Isa.56:7). This is a huge surprise to most Believers. Most have assumed that prayer will no longer be relevant as we will have Jesus present, right?

Wrong. There will be dynamic prayer meetings in the age to come. Communion and intimacy with God will be the primary passion and pursuit of Believers in the age to come.

> *Therefore with joy you will draw water from the wells of salvation. (4) And in that day you will say: Praise the LORD, call upon His name; declare His deeds among the peoples, make mention that His name is exalted (Isa.12:3-4)*

> *It shall come to pass that before they call, I will answer; and while they are still speaking, I will hear (Isa.65:24)*

> *Prayer also will be made for Him continually, and daily He shall be praised (Ps.72:15)*

> *The inhabitants of one city shall go to another, saying, Let us continue to go and pray before the LORD, and seek the LORD of hosts. (22) Yes, many peoples and strong nations shall come to seek the LORD of hosts in Jerusalem, and to pray before the LORD (Zech.8:21-22)*

We will join with our heavenly intercessor (Rom.8:34) and will use prayer as a means of both personal communion and as a wonderful help in assisting us to achieve supernatural breakthroughs during the reconstruction phase of the Millennial Kingdom. As we cry out and bring things before Him in prayer, Jesus will astound us with the speed in which He responds (Isa.65:24). Prayer will be one of the primary activities in the age to come.

We talk much about prayer in our churches today, however, our scandalously poor attendance at the actual prayer meetings betrays our lack of understanding about prayer. Prayer has always been and will continue to be, God's primary means of establishing His Kingdom rule and authority on earth. Ever wonder why today's church is so spiritually weak and complacent? Ever wonder why so many saints are bound and continue to remain bound in darkness? Ever wondered why Jesus taught His disciples to pray the way He did?

> *Your kingdom [Millennial Kingdom] come.*
> *Your will be done on earth as it is in heaven*
> *(Matt.6:10)*

If today's church had even a thimble full of revelation about what prayer releases and establishes when it is taken seriously, prayer rooms would be filled night and day. We'd build houses of prayer before we'd build new sanctuaries. Our cities would be on fire with a spirit of revelation. Sickness and disease would be driven from our midst. There would be a fresh spirit of cooperation among the various ministries in our cities instead of the selfish desire for our own ministries to grow and prosper. The legitimate needs of the poor would be met with no need for government assistance. Our youth would be fiery intercessors and evangelists instead of bored with church and looking in other places for their desires to be satisfied.

Until we get desperate enough to seek the Lord in earnest, distractions will continue to plague us. United corporate prayer has always been and will always be God's method of choice to release righteous government on the earth. This holds true in this age and will be true in the age to come as well. Lip service will do nothing to provide the changes we are longing to see in our own hearts, in the lives of our families and our communities. Someone aptly said, *"To the church without compromise, He will give His Spirit without measure."*

We have language but little reality of the things we profess. We have awesome forms but lack meaningful substance. We can share the stories of others but have little power or authority ourselves. We will remain impotent and spiritually feeble until our level of desperation surpasses our desires for worldly substitutes. We overdose on entertainment and recreation to try and camouflage our shallow spiritual existence rather than run to the One who can bring our much-needed cure. Fervent prayer is our solution and until it is rediscovered, our secret sins will keep us bound in silent oppression. That is a sad state of affairs, especially when *the Deliverer* stands patiently waiting for an invitation to help. We have not because we ask not (Ja.4:2).

I am not trying to be negative for no reason. I burn with desire to be part of an empowered church and can't stand to wait for another age to have that desire satisfied. I hope this appeal moves your heart and I hope even more, that it moves you to pray. We are in a desperate circumstance and it is growing more serious by the hour. What happened on 9/11, in Indonesia and in New Orleans are God's appeals for a sleeping church to arise and pray.

If that last statement offends you, I would encourage you to get a deeper foundation in the Word of God. Why do I say this? I mention this because the storm that is forming on the distant horizon will totally confound you if you are not spiritually apprised of these matters. God has a contention with America and will not pardon our iniquity because we are the *"strongest"* nation on earth. That only serves to make us that much more accountable. He cannot wink at the shedding of innocent blood. America is guilty to the tune of over 50,000,000 and that number is rising daily. When will enough blood be spilled to arouse His anger and prompt a sleepy church to pray (2 Chron.7:14)? Where are those He has called to cry out day and night in order to avert national tragedy?

> *So I sought for a man among them who would make a wall, and stand in the gap before Me on behalf of the land, that I should not destroy it; but I found no one. (31) Therefore I have poured out My indignation on them; I have consumed them with the fire of My wrath; and I have recompensed their deeds on their own heads, says the Lord GOD*
> *(Ezek.22:30-31)*

Prayer is God's remedy now and it will be the weapon of choice in the age to come as well. It should bring us comfort to know that Jesus is engaged in fervent prayer right now for his church (Heb.7:25). He understands that the promises of heaven must be activated by a willing participant on the earth for them to have their desired impact. His prayers are for a praying church to be stirred and to arise.

The Jews Restored to a Place of Prominence

Another massive subject that will take the Gentile church totally off-guard is the role that the Jewish Believers will have in the coming age. Without a spirit of revelation, what I am preparing to share with you, especially if you are a Gentile, will most likely create some level of offense. I feel compelled to share these things and would ask you to appeal to the Holy Spirit for keen discernment about these matters.

The Jewish people were God's primary choice through whom to reveal His redemptive plans. He intended to raise up a people who would so embody His Word that the entire earth would be forced to take note. Besides a momentary glimpse of that potential as seen during the beginning of King Solomon's reign, very little of that potential was ever witnessed by a lost Gentile world. God's plan in choosing the Jewish people was always for the purpose of world redemption (Deut.7:6-8). They never quite seemed to grasp the significance of their call, but God certainly is not finished with them as a nation. During the age to come, much of what they misunderstood will be restored. They will receive a fresh call and will operate under a renewed mandate during His Millennial Kingdom. Ezekiel 36:17-27 are stunning verses on this subject and worth reading.

There has always been a believing remnant of Jewish people on the earth (1 Kings 19:18). However, as a whole, they have been extremely resistant and often have played an adversarial role in regards to the gospel. The

Believing Gentiles are not without sin in this matter either, as we have a history of mistreating the Jewish people. Because of these injustices, the Jews have had no where to look for spiritual substance.

The Jews' relationship to Jesus and participation in His manifest kingdom will undergo a massive transformation in the coming age. I call this change of status, *the great reversal*. These staunch enemies of the gospel (Rom.11:28) suddenly become passionate lovers of their Messiah. This radical change appears to occur at the final moments of this current age. After the church is caught-up to meet Jesus in the air during the Second Coming Processional (1 Thess.4:15-17) Jesus returns to the Mount of Olives as prophesied (Acts 1:9-11). The Jewish remnant sees Him in the sky and begins to cry out to Him for deliverance and salvation. The Apostle Paul declares that the entire nation of Israel will experience salvation simultaneously (Rom.11:26). Numerous Old Testament scriptures testify to this as well (Zech.12:10).

Jesus then provides a supernatural way of escape for this Jewish remnant. He begins to deal harshly and decisively with those who have assembled to destroy the Jews and make war with Him (Zech.14:4,12; Rev.19:19).

This next portion of scripture is challenging. Even though I believe it is clear, I am not sure exactly how and when it will be played out. My best guess is that it occurs: (1) after the church is raptured (1 Thess.4:15-17) (2) after the Believers (Jewish and Gentile) receive their rewards (1 Cor.3:13-15) (3) after the Marriage Supper of the Lamb (Rev.19:9) (4) after the Second Coming Processional arrives in Jerusalem (Acts 1:9-11) (5) after Jesus slays those gathered to fight against Him (Zech.14:12) and (6) just prior to Jesus coming and setting up His Millennial headquarters in Jerusalem (Ez.40-48).

> *I will bring you out from the peoples and gather you out of the countries where you are scattered, [all Jews still alive throughout the nations of the earth] with a mighty hand, with an outstretched arm, and with fury poured out. (35) And I will bring you into the wilderness of the peoples, [this could perhaps be the wilderness sanctuary where the Jews who were supernaturally hidden by the Lord during the Great Tribulation have been camped - Rev.12] and there I will plead My case with you face to face. (36) Just as I pleaded My case with your fathers in the wilderness of the land of Egypt, so I will plead My case with you," says the Lord GOD. (37) "I will make you pass under the rod and I will bring you into the bond of the covenant; (38) I will purge the rebels from among you, and those who transgress against Me; I will bring them out of the country where they dwell, but they shall not enter the land of Israel [This seems reminiscent of those who rebelled against God in the wilderness under Moses leadership and who God removed with extreme judgments – Jude 11]. Then you will know that I am the LORD*
> *(Ezek.20:34-38)*

The reason this portion of scripture is important is that this is God's final purge of the Jewish people. Jesus handles this personally and I seriously doubt that any Gentile Believers will be permitted to attend this solemn event. This reminds me of a loving Father needing to deal with a few of His wayward children. It seems like it could be a closed family affair and will most likely be handled by Jesus in private with His covenant people, the Jews (Jer.31:35-37). I have a hunch that this next verse refers to this family gathering. It seems that the *"You who have followed me"* is referring to the twelve Apostles, who are Jewish, and will be assigned an active role in making spiritual assessments concerning their Jewish brothers and sisters. I believe this refers to the Apostles because the Bible mentions specifically *"twelve thrones"* from which His people will be judged.

> *So Jesus said to them, "Assuredly I say to you, that in the regeneration, [clearly a reference to the next age] when the Son of Man sits on the throne of His glory, you who have followed Me will also sit on twelve thrones, judging the twelve tribes of Israel (Matt.19:28)*

Anyway, after all the family matters get ironed out, the Jews who are now reconciled to Jesus will be major players in the age to come. The interesting thing is that some of them will have glorified bodies because they were born-again prior to Jesus' Second Coming Processional (i.e. 144,000 – Rev.7:4). Others will turn to the Lord moments before the age expires, but too late to be glorified (1

Cor.15:51-52). I hope I didn't lose or confuse you with all the details.

This is the main thing you need to know. Those who have received Jesus as Lord prior to the sounding of the seventh trumpet will receive a glorified body. Those who are born-again after that time (i.e. the resistors and their offspring – <u>if they convert</u>, and the Jewish Tribulation survivors along with their offspring – <u>if they convert</u>) will not receive glorified bodies until the next transition period when the New Jerusalem ascends from heaven (Rev.3:12; 21:2). We will touch on this later.

Quick note to reader: Even though I added the *"if they convert"* phrase after "the Jewish Tribulation Survivors and their offspring", I believe that the Bible is clear that the Jewish remnant and their offspring will never again deny their Messiah. I added that as a safety-net. I am 99.9% sure it will never be needed.

So the Millennial Kingdom will be occupied by Jewish and Gentile Believers with glorified bodies. Also, there will be new Jewish Believers without glorified bodies, as well as Gentile resistors who refused to take the Mark of the Beast. Jesus will allow these resistors to enter His kingdom as a reward for the courage they displayed in refusing to yield to the pressure placed on them and their families by the Antichrist. For these reasons, Jesus will extend to them a special exemption of grace. So what does this look like?

> For behold, I create Jerusalem as a rejoicing, and her people a joy. *(19)* I will rejoice in Jerusalem, and joy in My people;

> *The voice of weeping shall no longer be heard in her, nor the voice of crying. (21) They shall build houses and inhabit them; They shall plant vineyards and eat their fruit (22) They shall not build and another inhabit; They shall not plant and another eat; for as the days of a tree, so shall be the days of My people, and My elect shall long enjoy the work of their hands. (23) They shall not labor in vain, nor bring forth children for trouble; for they shall be the descendants of the blessed of the LORD, and their offspring with them*
> *(Isa.65:18-19;21-23)*

There is a wealth of information contained in these verses. However, the main thing I want you to see is that this passage of scripture is addressed to His Jewish survivors. They are in Jerusalem and they are in a total restoration mode. They are rebuilding homes that were destroyed during the various battles fought by the Antichrist in his failed attempts to seize control of Jerusalem. They are also involved in farming the land to produce food for their families.

A very important statement is the one concerning producing and raising children. This is specifically a function of those who have not yet received glorified bodies (Mk.12:35). These are clearly Jewish residents who were born-again during the Battle for Jerusalem and after the seventh trumpet (1 Cor.15:51-52). They will receive their glorified bodies at the end of the Millennial Reign of Christ.

The Jews will clearly be assigned roles of great authority and prominence during this 1,000-year reign.

> *Thus says the LORD of hosts: In those days*
> *ten men from every language of the nations*
> *shall grasp the sleeve of a Jewish man,*
> *saying, Let us go with you, for we have heard*
> *that God is with you*
> *(Zech.8:23)*

This is really quite an odd little verse and it had me totally mystified for years. I had no grid in which to place or process this, as all my Bible verses needed to apply before the Second Coming. Once you begin to understand the Millennial Kingdom, you will be completely shocked at the hundreds of verses that now make sense. Most have partial application now but will have substantial fulfillment in the ages to come as well. God knows how to get great mileage out of His Word.

CHAPTER 20

Jerusalem Receives a New Name

Another fascinating thing will be the changes God makes in the animal kingdom during the Millennial Age. Just like before the fall of man in Genesis 3, man experienced long life and enjoyed a friendly relationship with his surroundings, including the animals that he oversaw. God has plans to restore man's relationship with Himself and also repair the damage to the natural environment. Sin produced negative consequences in both. Take a look.

> *The wolf and the lamb shall feed together, the lion shall eat straw like the ox, and dust shall be the serpent's food. They shall not hurt nor destroy in all My holy mountain (Isa.65:25)*

> *The cow and the bear shall graze; their young ones shall lie down together; and the lion shall eat straw like the ox. (8) The nursing child shall play by the cobra's hole, and the weaned child shall put his hand in the viper's den. (9) They shall not hurt nor destroy in all My holy mountain (Isa.11:7-9)*

Aren't these verses fascinating?   There will be absolutely no fear or intimidation between humans and animals in the coming age. It will be forbidden by Jesus and you can count on that law being maintained. There is a possibility that this may be geographic-specific but I hope not. The *"holy mountain"* mentioned here is specifically a section of Jesus' Millennial Complex. It occupies about a ten-mile square tract of land and will house a unique company of saints (Ez.40-48). I am putting in my request now that the ban on hostile creatures will be expanded globally. I really don't like snakes.

Many today have pointed out the incredible crop production in Israel and have attributed this to her advanced irrigation systems. This has enabled her to produce much from little. She is able to do this with little space, little time and little water. As the world marvels at Jewish ingenuity, do not for a moment mistake their current measure of success as the high water mark of their achievement. The blessing that God is getting ready to release on their land is nothing less than miraculous. During the Millennial Kingdom the entire land of Israel will reach pre-curse vegetation status (i.e. Garden of Eden). To the nations, this will be a testimony of God's favor on a land that has suffered and seen so much hardship.

> *I will call for the grain and multiply it, and bring no famine upon you. (30) And I will multiply the fruit of your trees and the increase of your fields, so that you need never again bear the reproach of famine among the nations*
> *(Ezek. 36:29-30)*

> *On the day **that I cleanse you from all your iniquities…** (34) The desolate land shall be tilled instead of lying desolate in the sight of*

*all who pass by. (35) So they will say, This land that was desolate has become **like the garden of Eden*** *(Ezek.36:33-35)*

*And the desert shall rejoice and blossom as the rose; (2) **It shall blossom abundantly*** *(Isa.35:1-2)*

*Then the nations which are left all around you shall know that I, the LORD, have **rebuilt the ruined places** and planted what was desolate* *(Ezek.36:36)*

The Great Commission

A truly surprising feature of Jesus' Millennial Kingdom will be the continuation of the *"Great Commission"* (Matt.28:18-20). Jesus' passion to reach lost souls does not subside simply because there has been a transition from one age to the next. His heart still burns for the lost.

But, beloved, do not forget this one thing, that with the Lord one day is as a thousand years, and a thousand years as one day. (9) The Lord is not slack concerning His promise, as some count slackness, but is longsuffering toward us, <u>not willing that ANY should perish but that ALL should come to repentance</u> *(2 Pet.3:8-9)*

This is the heart of Jesus for every single citizen of His Millennial Kingdom. He does not want to see one who is lost or who will not make it safely to the New Jerusalem. Much will be done to assure that those who have not yet made a personal commitment to Christ will do so before Satan is loosed near the end of the Millennial Kingdom age (Isa.65:20). Remember, Jesus will not violate an individual's free will, so those who come to faith will do so with the aid of *Millennial Evangelistic Teams*. The Bible gives us an awesome picture of what this will look like.

> *Peoples shall yet come, inhabitants of many cities; (21)* **the inhabitants of one city shall go to another,** *saying,* **let us continue to go and pray before the LORD, and seek the LORD of hosts.** *I myself will go also. (22) Yes, many peoples and strong nations shall come to seek the LORD of hosts in Jerusalem and* **to pray before the LORD**
> *(Zech.8:20-22)*

You don't have to look too far to understand the spiritual dynamics of what is taking place here. Believers are gathering and then traveling to various cities to pray for God's favor. Souls are always the top priority in God's economy, so why is the emphasis on prayer rather than a well-organized outreach program? Why aren't they meeting together and talking about their various evangelistic strategies for reaching the lost? Why? Because they remember the hours and days spent planning big outreach events and the seconds and minutes spent praying over those elaborate plans. They also have not forgotten about the pathetic results because of a lack of prayer. Most of our areas of ministry ineffectiveness reflect the current prayerlessness in today's church. Jesus will personally disciple us as to how to impact entire cities. His strategies will always contain a high saturation of prayer.

The World's Revival Center

It also appears that many nations will send delegations of intercessors to Jerusalem to receive special training and equipping. Why Jerusalem? What's happening in Jerusalem that has the focus of the whole world? In the age to come Jerusalem will be the revival center of the entire earth. It will be full of the glory of the Lord. Take a glimpse.

> *And the ransomed of the LORD shall return, and* **come to Zion with singing**, *with everlasting joy on their heads.* **They shall obtain joy and gladness,** *and sorrow and sighing shall flee away*
> *(Isa.35:10)*

Catch the spirit of what is being communicated here. Mount Zion is another name for Jerusalem in the Bible. Jerusalem is where Jesus has chosen to set up His governmental headquarters. That massive complex is located in what Ezekiel calls "the district" (Ez.45:3). The district is an area that occupies roughly ten square miles. These are ten power-packed square miles, I might add. Jesus' Millennial Temple is located in this area and guess where Jesus' seat of government is located? Jesus governs the entire earth from the prayer room located in the Holy of Holies (Ez.48:8b,10b,12,14b,35b)! Is that spectacular or what! Guess what the name of the city of Jerusalem will become after Jesus sets up His throne in the Holy of Holies? The city from that time on will be named, *"THE LORD IS THERE"* (Ez.48:35b). Isn't that fantastic?

Now you can see why everyone can't wait to make a trip to Jerusalem. This city will be a city full of the joy of the Lord. When pilgrims from the nations gather for regularly scheduled celebrations (Zech.14:16) they will come with a heart that is overflowing with joy and gladness. The spirit of excitement and anticipation that these pilgrims will possess defies description as it will far surpass anything this current age has to offer. The rumors of those who have heard Jesus speak in person will add an air of exhilaration to this already ecstatic crowd.

The city itself will be the most glorious city you have ever seen. Words are totally inadequate to describe what we are going to be looking at on a daily basis in the age to come. Here is a quick snapshot of the magnificent landscape we will be seeing.

> *Great is the LORD, and greatly to be praised in the city of our God, in His holy mountain. (2)* ***Beautiful in elevation***, *the joy of the whole earth, is Mount Zion on the sides of the north, the city of the great King. (3)* ***God is in her palaces***; *He is known as her refuge. (4) For behold, the kings assembled, they passed by together. (5) They saw it, and so* ***they marveled***; *they were* ***troubled***, *they* ***hastened away***. *(6)* ***Fear took hold of them*** *there, and pain, as of a woman in birth pangs, (7) as when You break the ships of Tarshish with an east wind. (8) As we have*

*heard, so we have seen in the city of the
LORD of hosts, in the city of our God: God
will establish it forever. Selah
(Ps.48:1-8)*

I want you to use your sanctified imagination and
get a clear picture of what the Holy Spirit is trying to
communicate in this glorious description of the Millennial
Jerusalem, now called *"The Lord Is There,"* (Ez.48:35).
This is completely profound. You and I will actually be
staring at this one day and probably reacting much like
these kings of the earth. Their first reaction is that they are
awestruck ("marveled"). Then as the reality of what they
are seeing starts to grip their hearts they come under such
overwhelming conviction that they flee in terror. Why?
Because the Spirit of Holiness fills the entire atmosphere
surrounding this city, that's why. Look at their reaction.
This is real folks. You are not seeing some kind of science
fiction portrayal here. This is how stunning this city will be
and it will have a profound impact of those who visit. Can
you imagine what these kings tell their nations upon
returning from their ministry trip to attend one of Jesus'
three-day seminars? They had heard all the wild rumors but
now they have had first hand experience and are totally
amazed.

The Sky's the Limit

Did you catch the, *"Beautiful in elevation,"* part?
After Jesus returns to the Mount of Olives, the entire region
around Jerusalem experiences a massive topography
change. A large mountainous area that currently surrounds
Jerusalem goes flat and is turned into a plain and Jerusalem

itself gets substantially elevated (Zech.14:10). It's very possible that through all the radical topographical changes the earth has experienced during the horrific judgments of the Great Tribulation, Jerusalem may now be the highest elevation on earth. Remember, mountains were shaken and many, if not all, have fallen (Isa.2:19).

Not only is this city highly elevated, but also it is completely stunning to behold. The first thing that will catch your eye when approaching this magnificent city is its unsurpassed beauty. Think of the most gorgeous mountain landscape you have ever seen and then magnify that by ten. Jesus' mountain city will stop everyone in his tracks who catches a glimpse of it.

Once you recover from the shock and awe of that scene, the next feature that will grip your heart is the intimidating height of this mountain city. Who knows, it might even surpass Mt. Everest. Remember, Mt. Everest may no longer exist as we know it today. The sheer height of this glorious mountain will cause tour buses to stop and all the occupants to shout, "Glory to God," when they just get a peak at this splendid mountain city.

> *Now it shall come to pass in* **the latter days** *that the mountain of the LORD's house shall be established on the top of the mountains, and shall be* **exalted above the hills** *(Isa.2:2)*

The third and most awesome feature about this mountain will be the manifest presence of God that will overwhelm every single visitor. It is impossible to visit this city and not be physically, emotionally and spiritually impacted. The mere sight will stun you and then His presence will pierce your heart like a knife. Spontaneous worship will erupt from those who view this awesome sight. Those whose hearts are not quite right will flee in absolute terror, like the kings that Psalm 48 describes. No one can visit this Holy Mountain and be unmoved. He will either worship or flee, gripped with holy fear. Pride will not stand a chance. The proud will be instantly humbled and brought low (Isa.40:4). So what happens on this mountain?

> *Many people shall come and say, Come, and let us go up to the mountain of the LORD, to the house of the God of Jacob;* **He will teach us His ways**, *and we shall walk in His paths. For out of Zion [Jerusalem] shall go forth the law, and the word of the LORD from Jerusalem*
> *(Isa.2:3)*

Jesus Millennial Seminars

Most of us have been familiar with this passage for many years and had no paradigm for understanding the significant information contained in it. I used to envision myself in heaven, sitting with others in a large auditorium, listening to Jesus teach about life. Although this was wonderful, I saw no real correlation with my purpose or future destiny. Nor did these verses seem to have any relevance or relationship to my current life. I could not have been more mistaken.

Now I view this entire scene through an entirely different lens. Jesus' teaching ministry during the coming age is absolutely essential. Please do not limit His instruction to morality and biblical truth. His training sessions will cover a wide variety of issues. Jesus will be imparting understanding about every facet of our new lives in His kingdom. Certainly, He will teach us about morality and describe in great detail things that caused former generations so much heartache. He will help us understand why His commands are so important for us to follow. Remember, there will be many new Believers in attendance at these seminars. There will also be those still making spiritual decisions and weighing heavily the words Jesus will be sharing.

There is something we need to discuss at this juncture. It concerns the saints in glorified bodies and will be a great surprise for many who have received little or no teaching on the subject. It regards personal revelation. Most Christians assume that when they see Jesus they will suddenly understand some of the deep mysteries of the kingdom. They will be surprised when they discover that godly wisdom and understanding are both progressive and are acquired on an individual basis. Not everyone will have the same level of spiritual maturity in the age to come. Believers who have not taken their faith seriously will not be instantly knowledgeable about the things of God. God's kingdom operates on the principle of increase. The Bible says that, *"The increase of His government ... there will be no end"* (Isa.9:7). No one skips steps. It's always, *"Precept must be upon precept ... line upon line, here a little, there a little ..."* (Isa.28:10). Jesus was not exaggerating when He prophesied that, *"The meek would inherit the earth"* (Matt.5:5).

Seventy Year Internship

Our current life and ministry is like a seventy-year internship. How we live before God in meekness and love will pay huge dividends in the age to come. There will be individuals who have mega ministries during their earthly internship but will have little to show for it in the age to come. The movements of our hearts are closely monitored by God (Ps.139:1-3). Ministry success will have absolutely no value if it wasn't done in meekness and with a loving spirit. *"The last shall be first and the first last"* (Matt.20:16). Those operating with servants' hearts will receive much greater attention and reward from God than those who have obtained much but possess a prideful spirit. They may have succeeded in the eyes of men but lack the authorization and the approval of heaven (Matt.7:21-23). Your status and attainment in God on this side will be carried over and activated on the other side. I am mentioning this because I want you to understand that there is continuity between this present age and the next.

Jesus' teaching ministry will be a form of on-going discipleship. He will be correcting many of our false assumptions concerning kingdom principles. He will teach us about establishing our hearts in meekness and love. The good news is that it appears that those who attend His seminars really connect with what He shares. Isaiah says that not only will we be taught His ways but we will also *"Walk in His ways"* (Isa.2:3). That implies that we receive what He is teaching and then go out and apply those principles in our lives. I know of no greater compliment a Bible teacher can receive than for those who are taught, to then go and put into practice what they have received.

Please do not limit Jesus' teaching ministry to simple instruction about spiritual truths. Remember, the One who is teaching these classes is the same One who 6,000 years prior, spoke, and then multiple universes full of stars, planets, suns and moons were instantly created. He knows physics. He fully comprehends science. He knows agriculture and He knows government. He knows construction and engineering. He knows mathematics. He knows marine biology. He knows economics. He knows music. He knows art. He knows astronomy. He knows every detail about human bodies. Jesus is beyond brilliant. He is an expert in every field and His expertise in all these fields will be essential for the earth to be restored and maintained. He will unlock mysteries in many fields that will dazzle and amaze those with doctorate degrees.

Some fields are one key idea away from critical breakthroughs. Jesus is full of dynamic ideas and will stun the experts with His grasp of their chosen profession. He's more than a Bible teacher. He is literally the master of the universe. He knows every answer to every problem in existence. He knows how to do it, when it needs to be done and understands the simplest and fastest way to get the task completed. In short, He is awesome!

I want you to understand the scope of the little phrase, *"He will teach us His ways."* Although this sentence only contains six words, believe me, it covers the entire spectrum of life. Jesus' teaching ministry will be both comprehensive and extremely practical. He is more than a theologian; He is a fully qualified instructor on every area of life. Indeed, He will teach us His ways and because of that, our lives will be greatly enhanced.

He shall judge between the nations, and rebuke many people*; they shall beat their swords into plowshares, and their spears into pruning hooks; nation shall not lift up sword against nation,* **neither shall they learn war anymore**
(Isa.2:4)

The Lord is at Your right hand; He shall ***execute kings*** *in the day of His wrath.* *(6) He shall judge among the nations,* ***He shall fill the places with dead bodies, He shall execute the heads of many countries***
(Ps.110:5-6)

Jesus has three primary role assignments in redemptive history. He's a Bridegroom (intimacy), He's a King (authority) and He is also a Judge (justice). One of the first things that Jesus will do after His return is to bring together all those who were given places of authority and have them give an account of their leadership. Wicked and corrupt heads of state will be rounded up, tried and summarily executed for war crimes against God and humanity (Ps.110:5-6). It will be similar to the Nuremberg war tribunals held after World War II. It took over a year to round up the guilty parties, bring them to justice and pass the appropriate sentence. Jesus will do basically the same thing. Psalm 2 should be memorized by every person in governmental leadership worldwide. Those given much will be responsible for much. Many will be executed on the spot. This is not a time of mercy; this is God's hour of Justice. Dead bodies will be lying everywhere as Jesus personally removes all wicked leaders. Some will be commended. Some will be rebuked but allowed to live. Others will experience the sword of the Lord (Rev.1:16). Justice will be swift and totally accurate (Mal.3:5).

This side of Jesus makes many Christians extremely uncomfortable. Their discomfort exposes their unfamiliarity with the judicial-face of Jesus. This is the reason why today, when God releases His justice even in limited ways, the Body of Christ is greatly perplexed and confused. Some are even embarrassed. Many current examples of His justice are blamed on the devil. We cannot bear to think that God would actually send natural disasters as a means to get our attention and try to motivate a sleepy church to pray (2 Chron.7:14). He is full of mercy and compassion, but He is also a God of justice. He can pour out wrath and in the midst of that horrific act extend mountains of mercy. He doesn't have to suspend one attribute in order to release another. He is both a Bridegroom and a Judge. He has a contention with the nations of the earth and His judgments are for the purpose of removing everything that hinders love. The end time judgments are God's weapons of love that will be released to humble mankind so it can return to the Lord. Unfortunately, many will harden their hearts and experience the full measure of His displeasure.

Most Believers have so romanticized the Second Coming that they miss the fact that it will usher in the bloodiest time in the history of mankind, and it's the Son of God who will be responsible for all the carnage (Isa.63). This next portion of scripture is literal. This is not Jesus speaking symbolically. Read Isaiah 63 if you want graphic details. This is our Judge in action at the end of the age. We need to understand this face of Jesus because the wicked will feel the fullness of His anger. Never forget that the Lamb of God is also the Lion of Judah. We love it when we see Him manifest His kindness and tender mercies. But make no mistake about it, when this Lamb comes, He will shake the foundations of the earth as He roars from Zion (Joel 3:16).

> *The LORD shall go forth like a mighty man; He shall stir up His zeal like a man of war. He shall cry out, yes, shout aloud; He shall prevail against His enemies. (14) Promise of the LORD's Help. I have held My peace a long time, I have been still and restrained Myself. Now I will cry like a woman in labor, I will pant and gasp at once. (15) I will lay waste the mountains and hills, and dry up all their vegetation; I will make the rivers coastlands, and I will dry up the pools (Isa.42:13-15)*

CHAPTER 21

The Corridor of Glory

This next section will be unusual and I offer it as food for thought. Many biblical researchers have struggled for explanations when trying to define where the saints with glorified bodies will live. It is very clear that the inhabitants of the kingdom age who have natural bodies will build houses, work the land (as well as other employment) and raise families. But what about those in glorified bodies? We know some of what these bodies can do as Jesus modeled this for us after the resurrection. I touched on that earlier. In short, these new bodies are real and tangible. They will look like us. They have the capacity to consume and digest food. They are extremely mobile and can move from one location to another instantly. They don't get tired so they require no sleep. They are able to walk through walls. They can appear and then just as quickly disappear. They will be awesome and extremely efficient.

So where do those with glorified bodies go when those in natural bodies need to spend time with their families and get rested? Do we have special housing? If so where is it?

Jesus, when asked a question concerning marriage in the age to come said this, *"In the resurrection they neither marry nor are given in marriage, but are like angels of God in heaven"* (Matt 22:30). This was a new paradigm to those who heard Jesus share that brief statement. In the resurrection we are totally consumed with serving Jesus and loving God. Marriage will be unnecessary. I understand that this immediately concerns some, but please resolve that there are some of God's mysteries that we will not understand on this side of glory. It will all make sense then, and for now we must simply make this an issue of trust and faith. We will come into total agreement with His plans then, because our capacity to understand the will of God will be substantially increased.

If our new glorified bodies give us angelic capabilities, then do we go to heaven while our friends in natural bodies visit with their families and sleep? Let me propose a solution that may seem pretty extreme but many Bible researchers believe this to be true and they support it with scripture.

At the end of the Millennial Kingdom, the earth is purged (2 Peter 3:12) and is replaced by the New Jerusalem. God has promised that He will establish His Kingdom on the earth, in Jerusalem, forever (Ps.48:8). We will talk about the specifics of New Jerusalem shortly. For the sake of our current discussion, the New Jerusalem will be much larger and much more dynamic than the Millennial Kingdom it replaces. The general location remains the same but it has many new features and realms of glory.

Heavenly Convergence

Many scholars believe that before the New Jerusalem descends fully to earth as seen by the Apostle John (Rev.21:2), that it hovers above the Millennial Kingdom and the two are dynamically connected by what Mike Bickle has called, *"the Corridor of Glory!"* What a descriptive title. Allow what I just described to settle for a moment in your heart. This adds new meaning to Paul's words in the Book of Ephesians. Remember, this is one of the foundational keys that we have been given to unlock and understand the millennial paradigm.

> *Having made known to us **the mystery of His** **will**, according to His good pleasure which He purposed in Himself, (10) that in the dispensation of the fullness of the times He **might gather together in one all things in** **Christ, both which are in heaven and which** **are on earth** -- in Him*
> *(Eph.1:9-10)*

God's desire to bring both the heavenly realm and the earthly realm together will not reach its full expression until the New Jerusalem descends. However, it will be substantially enhanced during the Millennial Reign of His Son. The Corridor of Glory provides the necessary linkage between these two realities. Obviously, no one can clearly tell you the exact distance between the Millennial Jerusalem and the New Jerusalem, but it may or may not be a great distance. I have a hunch that the New Jerusalem will be visible to the naked eye, but it may not be. The Corridor of Glory will certainly be visible and will look much like the cloud of glory that rested over the Holy of Holies during the children of Israel's wilderness journey. It went straight up to heaven. The Millennial version of that cloud will be greatly enhanced and will serve as a spiritual umbilical cord between the two realms. The saints in glorified bodies will travel through this glorious corridor from the New Jerusalem to earth and back again. Like members of Congress who live outside Washington, D.C. but commute back and forth, so it will be in the Millennial Kingdom. You will love your commute in the coming age!

Biblical Reasoning

Let me give you five biblical reasons as to why I believe what I just described is true: (1) the kings of the earth are allowed to visit this realm and bring their glory (2) the New Jerusalem contains leaves for the healing of the nations and there is absolutely no sickness or disease permitted in heaven (3) there are angels posted to prevent the ungodly from entering the city (4) the New Jerusalem gives illumination to the earth and (5) glorified bodies have angelic qualities and angels abide in the manifest presence of the Lord.

> *The kings of the earth bring their glory and honor into it [New Jerusalem]*
> *(Rev. 21:24)*

This is an extremely interesting passage of scripture. Even though it doesn't provide an overwhelming amount of specific information, it does provide us with an insight that is nothing less than striking. It plainly shows that there is not only a connection but also an exchange taking place between the earthly realm and the heavenly realm. Kings of the earth are allowed to visit the New Jerusalem while still actively providing leadership in the Millennial Jerusalem. This is a glorious discovery. The *"Kings of the earth"* are saints in glorified bodies who are actively serving in positions of authority on the earth. Therefore, it seems reasonable that the New Jerusalem must be in fairly close proximity to the earth.

Trees with Healing Leaves

*In the middle of its street [in the New
Heavenly Jerusalem], and on either side of
the river, was the tree of life, which bore
twelve fruits, each tree yielding its fruit every
month. **The leaves of the tree were for the
healing of the nations***
(Rev.22:2)

Since there will be no need of healing in the New
Jerusalem, it stands to reason that these leaves are used
where they are most needed. I submit for your
consideration that these leaves are taken to the Millennial
Jerusalem to be used to help strengthen those living in
natural bodies. These leaves must contain properties that
produce healing and longevity to those on earth. The
Millennial Kingdom also contains trees that are useful for
healing. This is an interesting concept as we typically
ascribe all sickness to the devil. He is bound and is not an
issue until the close of the Millennial Kingdom. However,
there will be sinners present and that means that sin will
still have an effect. Where there is sin there is sickness.
Where there is sickness there will be a need for healing.
Although much of the healing will be done through prayer
and the laying on of hands (Ja.5:14-16), some apparently
will be done by these leaves that contain healing properties.

*Along the bank of the river, on this side and
that, will grow all kinds of trees used for
food; their leaves will not wither, and their
fruit will not fail. They will bear fruit every
month, because their water flows from the*

279

> sanctuary. ***Their fruit will be for food, and their leaves for medicine***
> *(Ezek.47:12)*

In the Millennial Kingdom there will be trees that are along the banks of this supernatural river. This river will flow from the Millennial Temple (Jesus' headquarters) to the Dead Sea. The Dead Sea instantly becomes alive with sea life. If you have ever visited the Dead Sea you will understand how bizarre this verse really is. The Dead Sea becomes a major fishing center in the Millennial Kingdom (Ez.47:8-10). I suggest you read the entire chapter of Ezekiel 47 as it contains many important pieces of information that I think you might find helpful.

My guess is that the leaves that are transferred from the New Jerusalem and used on earth will be used for those with the most severe needs. That is my speculation based on the information provided. If there are leaves for healing in the New Jerusalem, where there is absolutely no need, then it makes sense that these leaves be distributed on earth where those in natural bodies can use them. If the Millennial Kingdom also has leaves that are used for both food and health, there could only be a few reasons for this duplication. The premise I use when trying to solve these kinds of problems is that God always has purpose for everything He does, and everything He does is always for man's good. These are my thoughts: (1) one leaf could be stronger than the other (2) perhaps they contain different ingredients that cure different ailments and (3) the supply on earth could be limited and therefore more leaves are needed.

Heavenly Gates Well Protected

*Also she had a great and high wall with **twelve gates**, and twelve angels at the gates (Rev.21:12)*

Blessed are those who do His commandments ... and may enter through the gates into the city. (15) But outside are dogs and sorcerers and sexually immoral and murderers and idolaters, and whoever loves and practices a lie (Rev. 22:14-15)

There are angels that are posted by each of the twelve gates of the New Jerusalem. The only reason why there would be a need for them to be stationed at these gates would be for the purpose of security. They are certainly not placed there as window dressings. After all, this is not Buckingham Palace; this is the ultimate expression of the Kingdom of Heaven. The angels serve a purpose and it appears their purpose is to keep anyone with a defiled spirit from entering the New Jerusalem. Only those with proper authorization may enter. This may have been what Jesus was referring to in the parable in Matthew 22:11-13.These angels are messengers of God's mercy, for those who might try to enter without the proper spiritual authorization (i.e. glorified body) would be instantly slain by the glory in that environment. Moses had to be covered by the hand of God or he would have been instantaneously destroyed. The Bible's testimony concerning Moses is that he was the meekest man on the earth at that time. If a godly man must be protected lest he perish, how much more those who are ungodly? Just a thought.

> *The city had no need of the sun or of the moon to shine in it, for the glory of God illuminated it. The Lamb is its light. (24) And the nations of those who are saved shall walk in its light*
> *(Rev.21:23-24)*

There are two ways to look at these verses and both equally confirm the existence of the New Jerusalem hovering over the Millennial Kingdom. I will give you two different ways to approach this passage. One or possibly both might apply. These verses appear to be suggesting: (1) that the New Jerusalem has the capacity to provide supernatural illumination to selected portions of Jesus' Millennial Kingdom and (2) a select group of redeemed individuals (I assume this is specific to those in glorified bodies) are allowed entrance into the New Jerusalem to bask in its beauty.

Note to reader: If the first point holds true, this also may be implying that there will be a distinction made between the saved and the unsaved who are both in natural bodies. God may gather the saved into specific areas, regions or nations and have a point of separation between the two. The wheat and tares principle only has application during our current age (Matt.24-30). Also remember we are acting like spiritual CSI investigators. Sometimes we are given only small clues and we are trying to reach biblical conclusions based, at times, on extremely limited information. God loves us pondering these matters. (Pro.25:2).

*For in **the resurrection** they neither marry
nor are given in marriage, but **are like
angels of God in heaven***
(Matt.22:30)

Notice the connection between the resurrection, the
angels of God and where the angels are located. If we will
be like the angels of God after the resurrection, it is
reasonable that we will be abiding where they abide when
not serving humans on the earth. It seems to me that this is
a giant hint about what is to come.

Satan's Last Stand

*Now when the thousand years have expired,
Satan will be released from his prison (8) and
will go out **to deceive the nations** which are
in the four corners of the earth ... to gather
them together to battle, **whose number is as
the sand of the sea**. (9) They went up on the
breadth of the earth and surrounded the
camp of the saints and the beloved city. And
fire came down from God out of heaven and
devoured them. (10) The devil, who deceived
them, was cast into the lake of fire and
brimstone where the beast and the false
prophet are. And they will be tormented day
and night forever and ever*
(Rev.20:7-10)

Here is what I want us to know: (1) Satan is not
released from prison until the entire 1,000 years are

complete (2) he is given parole to see if his incarceration has produced any change (3) he immediately returns to his deceptive ways (4) he is successful in deceiving a large number of people (5) they gather to attack Jerusalem and to remove Jesus as their King (6) Jesus immediately puts down this short lived uprising and consumes them in His anger and (7) the devil is removed and sentenced to spend eternity in the Lake of Fire.

Satan has been incarcerated in the Bottomless Pit for a full 1,000 years. His sentence will not get shortened for good behavior nor does God offer him an early release program. He does the maximum amount of time. He then demonstrates that he has not learned anything in that 1,000-year season of confinement and immediately upon release returns to his deceptive patterns.

One of the biggest surprises of the coming age is how it ends. Those who cannot bring themselves to believe that Jesus allows unsaved individuals to populate that period of time have real problems here. There are only two classes of people on earth, those who are born-again and those who are not. If you remove the unsaved category from the age to come, you are left with Satan going out to deceive Christians who are executed in the final end time judgment. In addition to conflicting with scripture, that view makes no logical sense at all. I stand by my conclusion that there will be unbelievers who are swayed, and in the end, will choose to follow a persuasive fallen demon rather than give their allegiance to the King of glory.

A Theologian's View

Robert Govett, <u>*The Apocalypse Expounded by Scripture*</u>[6], suggests four reasons why Satan must be loosed after a thousand years: (1) to demonstrate that man even under the most favorable circumstances will fall into sin if left to his own choice (2) to demonstrate the foreknowledge of God who foretells the acts of men as well as His own acts (3) to demonstrate the incurable wickedness of Satan and (4) to justify eternal punishment, that is, to show the unchanged character of wicked people even under divine jurisdiction for a long period of time.

The Hidden Mystery

The question that most people have when they discover this scenario is, "How could any human possibly be with Jesus for 1,000 years and then choose to team-up with the devil?" That is a real perplexing question, however, the answer is not that tough. How many of you love a good mystery? God loves mysteries as well, which indirectly explains why humans are so captivated by a good mystery. There are at least nine different mysteries described in the New Testament. One of the most profound is called the "mystery of iniquity" or the *"Mystery of lawlessness"* depending on what translation you read (2 Thess.2:7). Paul tells us that this mystery was around during his tenure on earth so we can safely assume that this mystery has some pretty serious shelf-life. In fact, we learn that this mystery makes it all the way through the Millennial Age.

---

[6] Chas J Thynne, pp 629 *The Apocalypse Expounded by Scripture –* London 1920

This mystery allows humans who have rejected truth to easily accept lies. They are prime candidates for deception. Satan easily preys on these individuals just like old lions love to attack wounded animals.

The question then becomes, how do people who have been listening to Jesus speak for a 1,000 years, suddenly turn Him off and start listening to the devil? The answer is quite simple. They do it one step at a time. No one suddenly wakes up one day completely deceived. It occurs over a period of time by rejecting God's time-proven ways and putting in its place, man's thoughts and man's ways. It is not difficult to figure out.

There are individuals who would like to justify their lack of faith by saying to God, "If I could have seen you in person I would have surely believed in you." God's answer is, "That is not true. You would be just like those who spent 1,000 years listening to my Son and in the end, you would still choose to believe a lie." The Millennial Kingdom will offer irrefutable proof that His word is true and that many prefer to believe lies rather than follow Him (2 Thess.2:11).

I am sure Satan will tell them that Jesus is on a huge ego trip and wants everybody to worship Him because He loves to control and dominate people. He will convince them that Jesus is restricting them from reaching their full potential and doesn't want them to have fun. In the end the battle is always about pleasure. Are we going to allow God to become the ultimate pleasure in our lives or are we going to sell out for Satan's counterfeit pleasures. Both create life-changing addictions. Becoming addicted to God causes people to fast and pray in order to experience more of His love and to deepen our understanding of Him. Becoming addicted to various worldly vices causes people to loose everything, including their dignity and eventually their sanity. Which addiction are you pursuing?

Satan, although very successful in gathering a crowd, is completely unsuccessful in his attempt to seize Jesus' throne in Jerusalem. It takes the Holy Spirit less than half a verse in scripture to describe the devil's foiled plans. His army is destroyed in one swift move of God's wrath and Satan is immediately thrown into the Lake of Fire. His torment is forever. If you look up the word *"forever"* in the Greek dictionary you will discover that it means a really, really, really long time.

The Great White Throne Judgment

*Then I saw a great white throne and Him who sat on it, from whose face the earth and the heaven fled away. And there was found no place for them. (12) **And I saw the dead, small and great, standing before God**, and books were opened. And another book was opened, which is the Book of Life. And the dead were judged according to their works, by the things which were written in the books. (13) **The sea gave up the dead who were in it,** and Death and Hades delivered up the dead who were in them. And they were judged, each one according to his works. (14) Then Death and Hades were cast into the lake of fire. This is the second death. (15) And anyone not found written in the Book of Life was cast into the lake of fire*
(Rev.20:11-15)

I will not spend a lot of time on this because I think it is basically self-explanatory. The one thing you need to know is that there is almost unanimous agreement among scholars that this event is strictly for unbelievers. Believers were evaluated after the rapture of the church immediately following the seventh trumpet. This is the second resurrection and it is a sad state of affairs. Notice the scope of those who were gathered to participate in this judgment. Verse 12 makes it clear that neither class, nor rank, neither position nor standing in society will have any bearing on how you are judged. This text lets us know how complete this judgment will be by asserting that even those who perished at sea will be drawn out of the waters to stand trial (v.13). This is not an event that any should consider lightly as it will be the most serious matter imaginable. These individuals who have rejected Christ and are not found in the Book of Life will join the devil, his angels, the Antichrist and the False Prophet in the Lake of Fire. This internment is called the "*second death*" and is eternal.

The Believer's Judgment

This may seem like an odd place to insert an event that occurred during the Great Tribulation after the seventh trumpet sounded. I have done so only for the sake of comparison. I think it will be helpful to have these two extremely different events located in close proximity so the reader might see plainly the broad differences. Let's look at the verses that describe this event.

> **For we must all appear** before the judgment seat of Christ, that each one may receive the things **done in the body,** according to what

he has done, whether good or bad. (11)
Knowing, therefore, the terror of the Lord,
we persuade men; but we are well known to
God, and I also trust are well known in your
conscience
(2 Cor.5:10-11)

For no other foundation can anyone lay
than that which is laid, which is Jesus Christ.
(12) Now if anyone builds on this foundation
with gold, silver, precious stones, wood, hay,
straw, (13) **each one's work will become**
clear; *for the Day will declare it, because it*
will be revealed by fire; and **the fire will test**
each one's work, *of what sort it is. (14)* **If**
anyone's work which he has built on it
endures, **he will receive a reward**. *(15)* **If**
anyone's work is burned, he will suffer loss;
but he himself will be saved, yet so as
through fire
(1 Cor.3:11-15)

Several things I want you to notice: (1) we all must appear
(2) we are accountable for the good and the bad (3) God's
judgments should be a strong motivator for us to share
Christ with others (4) Jesus Christ will be the plumb line by
which we will be judged (5) how we lived our lives will
matter (6) our works will be evaluated by God (7) only
works done in agreement with His Word and His Spirit will
have value and (8) no one participating in this judgment
will experience eternal damnation but may suffer loss of
rewards.

The information contained in these verses is significant and needs to be clearly understood and greatly appreciated by every person who names Jesus as their Lord. First, no Believer will be excluded from this evaluation process. Attendance is mandatory and the Lord will make sure all His people are there. Second, personal responsibility will matter during this time. Like good stewards, this is our time of squaring our accounts with God. Third, knowing that we will one day give a full account to God should inspire us to tell others of His kindness and warn them of His wrath. Fourth, there is only one acceptable foundation for true faith and that is Jesus Christ. Those who attempt to blend different faiths to cover all their bases will not be present at this time. Fifth, the quality of our faith will be significantly more important to us at that moment than many have realized. Sixth, there will be a clear distinction made between things done in presumption and activities done by the leading of the Spirit. Seventh, although many will experience great loss at this time, no one is in danger of eternal separation or he/she would not be present.

Note to reader: (1) there will be many Believers who will fall away during the Great Tribulation and not only lose their rewards but will lose their claim of salvation (Matt.24:9-13; 2 Thess.2:3). To believe otherwise is to believe something not consistent with the Word of God. Jesus identifies what this looks like in Matthew 22:11-13. Hebrews 6:4-6 puts this as clearly as anywhere in the Word of God. This is a serious matter and should be prayerfully and soberly considered. (2) Rewards are given on the basis of faithful service and obedience at the heart level. Jesus is always concerned about the heart. Some are making a great display of their Christianity but in truth, much of their motivation is totally misguided. However, only Jesus can make these kinds of determinations. Men always judge by externals and God is always checking out the movements of our hearts. He is much more gracious than we believe and He will stun us with His kindness in that day. It seems that the intentions of our hearts are always greater than our life attainments. Jesus understands completely and evaluates us primarily based on our measure of humility, the way we expressed our love to Him and how we served others. (3) Many that are last now will be first then. Many hidden intercessors who had little or no esteem from men, will now receive much attention and great rewards in the coming age. Many who appeared to accomplish much through human strength and God-given abilities will have little to show for it later. God is a passionate God who closely monitors the movements of our hearts. (4) 1 Corinthians 15 makes it clear that just as the cosmos has great variety and glory, the same will be true of Believers after the resurrection. I believe that degrees of glory will be visible in the form of light and the brightness of spirit that will be reflected from our very countenance. God's favor will be manifested in many degrees and measured in light. Proximity to His throne will be the ultimate reward. Who will be closest and who will be the greatest distance away will be shocking. (5) Faithfulness in this life will be very important in the age to come and will determine who is given what responsibilities under Jesus' righteous reign.

CHAPTER 22

The New Jerusalem

I mentioned earlier that there were three levels of glory: (1) the glory of this age can best be described as *partial*; (2) the glory of the next age can best be described as *substantial*; and, (3) the glory of the final age can best be described as *the ultimate*.

> *Now I saw a new heaven and a new earth, for the first heaven and the first earth had passed away. Also there was no more sea. (2) Then I, John, saw the holy city, New Jerusalem, coming down out of heaven from God, prepared as a bride adorned for her husband. (3) And I heard a loud voice from heaven saying, Behold, the tabernacle of God is with men, and He will dwell with them, and they shall be His people. God Himself will be with them and be their God. (4) And God will wipe away every tear from their eyes; there shall be no more death, nor sorrow, nor crying. There shall be no more pain, for the former things have passed away.*
> *(Rev.21:1-4)*

Revelation 21-22 is without a doubt the most encouraging portion of scripture in the entire Bible. For centuries saints have found great comfort when facing overwhelming problems by receiving just a glimpse of what is pictured here. Please remember that this scene follows the Millennial Kingdom and marks the start of an entirely new and glorious age. The New Jerusalem will be populated only by Believers in glorified bodies. Although the Bible is silent on exactly how and when Believers in natural bodies receive their awesome up-grade, it most likely will take place immediately after Satan's final revolt and just prior to *The Great White Throne Judgment*. That is my best guess and seems to be a fitting place for such a glorious transition.

We are told that this city is huge (Rev.21:16). It is laid out in a square and is 1,500 miles long by 1,500 mile wide and is 1,500 in height. Some scholars have speculated that it is possible that the New Jerusalem could be shaped like pyramid. They base that theory on the measurements given in scripture. Since the Bible only provides us with basic length, width, and height dimensions, the city appears to be laid out in the shape of either a cube or a pyramid. We'll just have to wait and see.

Someone noted that if you were to overlay this city and place it within the borders of the United States it would roughly start at the west coast and extend across to the Mississippi River in the east, would extend up to the Canadian border in the north, and down to the border that separates Texas from Mexico in the south. The thing I want us to understand is that this city is larger than many current nations. This is certainly one super-sized city.

God Saves the Best for Last

With all the wonderful things we could mention about this impressive city, its most outstanding feature has nothing to do with its enormous size, questionable shape or some of its dazzling architectural characteristics. The most awesome thing about this city is who lives there. For the first time ever, we will be introduced to our heavenly Father. We will be well acquainted with His Son as we will have just spent 1,000 years watching and assisting Him in governing the nations of the earth. We will be as amazed with Jesus at the end of the Millennial Kingdom as we were when He began His reign over 1,000 years prior. His presence will never become something common or even ordinary. Being near Him will always be exhilarating and supernaturally exciting. We will experience the same invigorating presence that the four living creatures experience every time they capture a fresh glimpse of the One seated on the throne (Rev.4:8). They cannot restrain themselves from giving spontaneous worship and glory to the Father and the Son, and neither will we. We will understand worship not as something we simply do but as the highest expression of who we are. We were made as instruments of worship and through worldly defilement we lost our way. But that will be substantially restored during the millennial age and will be ultimately restored in the New Jerusalem.

Those who thought the worship services were about warming up the crowd so the important work of preaching could be done will have a fresh new revelation of how convoluted that type of thinking really was. Sounds of worship will be heard everywhere in the city.

> *And God will wipe away every tear from their eyes; there shall be no more death, nor sorrow, nor crying. There shall be no more pain, for the former things have passed away (Rev. 21:4)*

This verse is one of the most comforting verses in the entire Word of God. Every Believer I know is aware that this verse is in their Bibles. It is one of those verses when you first discover it, you just have to stare at it because it seems too good to be true. It gives us an understanding of the personality of God that we somehow overlook in other parts of scripture.

Flawed Theology

I do want to bring some clarification to this verse because a wrong view gives way to flawed theology. I have heard it mentioned that the reason God is wiping away tears from our eyes is because these are tears of regret. Supposedly, these poor saints are having bad thoughts about what could have been if they had lived their lives in a more dedicated way, thus they are greatly distressed. So God is walking through the crowd with Kleenex in hand wiping cheeks and bringing us comfort. That makes for a great sermon and will probably stir a congregation to have some sober thoughts about their lives but it doesn't accurately represent what is really taking place here.

The emphasis of this passage is about the comfort of God not the remorse of the saints. The key to having a right perspective on this passage is found at the end of the verse, *"The former things have passed away."* The Holy Spirit is letting us know that it's a new day. Please keep in mind that these are individuals who have been living in glorified bodies and ministering with Jesus for the last 1,000 years. Any regrets we might have had were dealt with centuries ago. The truth about the New Jerusalem that is being communicated here is that the old order of things is totally removed. The old earth has been replaced by a new earth. We do not suddenly find ourselves being catapulted through empty space in this pyramid shaped city, with no bearings. That's science fiction. What is transpiring here is both real and dynamic. The old earth, having fulfilled its purpose, is removed and is replaced by the new earth (2 Pet.3:10-13). The old heaven is also removed and is replaced by a new heaven. This new heaven differs greatly from the former heaven because there is no need for the sun to light up the daytime or the moon to give light in the night. The reason for this change is simple. Jesus will be reflecting the glory of His Father and that glorious light will be sufficient to light up the entire New Jerusalem. The moon will no longer be necessary because there is no night season in this city. The New Jerusalem, which has been suspended for the last 1,000 years above the old earth, for the first time, makes its descent and is positioned on this newly formed earth. This is the ultimate fulfillment of the verses in Ephesians that we have been using as our primary text throughout our study of the last days.

> *Having made known to us the mystery of His will, according to His good pleasure which He purposed in Himself,* (10) *that in the dispensation of the fullness of the **times He might gather together in one all things in Christ, both which are in heaven and which are on earth** -- in Him*
> *(Eph.1:9-10)*

His mystery is now both fully understood and will be experienced in its most comprehensive form. I am convinced that when Paul had his third-heaven experience that he was given a glimpse of much of the glory that John was permitted to record in the Book of Revelation. To accurately describe the glory that awaits the saints, Paul uses two composite verses taken from the Book of Isaiah. If you study these verses you will quickly discover that both are clearly embedded in a millennial context. Paul's encouragement to end time Believers is the following:

> *Eye has not seen, nor ear heard, nor have entered into the heart of man the things which God has prepared for those who love Him*
> *(1 Cor.2:9)*

This verse makes our heart leap and helps trigger our sanctified imaginations to meditate on how awesome our future inheritance in God really is. Like they say in the infomercials, ***"But wait, there's more!"***

> *But **God has revealed them to us through His Spirit**. For the Spirit searches all things, yes, the deep things of God*
> *(1 Cor.2:10)*

This is such a wonderful verse. Verse 9 leaves us with the impression that the things God plans to do in the future are totally beyond our ability to fathom. There is certainly a strong degree of truth in this statement. However, verse 10 suddenly offers us hope, at least in a partial sense, that some of the glory of the future age can be accessible and comprehensible in our present experience with God. That's all the motivation a gold-digger needs to keep him going for awhile. If we will apply our hearts to these things, God will download more living understanding of His end time plans than we can possibly imagine.

Paradigm Shift

Please stay with me as I try to explain this next truth. I honestly believe this can add a entirely new spark to your Bible study and the way you evaluate and interpret many scriptures. There are truths in the Word of God that stare us in the face every time we read our Bibles and we completely miss the greater understanding because we are operating with an old paradigm. With a slight adjustment in our thinking there is a new world of insight waiting to be discovered. Let me explain.

Please keep in mind the thing I have frequently repeated about the distinction between the various ages. Our current age is the partial. The millennial age is the substantial. The New Jerusalem is the ultimate. We learned that in the New Jerusalem God plans to bring an end to some things, *"For the former things have passed away"* (21:4). Immediately following that verse we are told, *"Behold, I make all things new"* (21:5). Next we hear Him say, *"It is done"* (21:6)! Now let me give you a very familiar verse to evaluate.

> *Therefore, if anyone is in Christ, he is a new creation;* ***old things have passed away; behold, all things have become new.***
> *(2 Cor.5:17-18)*

I can almost hear some of you saying, "Okay, where are you going with all this?" Without a deeper understanding of the future ages, a familiar verse like this only seems to have immediate and temporal application. However, when you place this verse in the broader context of the Millennial Kingdom, it has substantially more meaning and greater impact. When you move this all the way out to the New Jerusalem, we discover its ultimate fulfillment.

My point is that there are literally hundreds of verses that have this kind of progressive implication. If we keep these types of truths bound to their most immediate context we lose sight of the much broader picture. Does that make sense? I hope you are still following me as this can make a dramatic change in how you interpret the Word of God.

When Paul, writing under the inspiration of the Holy Spirit, mentions that, *"All things have passed away, behold, all things have become new,"* he completely understood that he was passing on progressive revelation. He was keenly aware that what he was imparting to future generations would have partial and immediate application during this current age. However, he also understood that these truths would have substantial application in the age to come and would find their ultimate fulfillment in the New Jerusalem. Try to imagine for a moment: (1) living every moment in a totally sinless environment (2) while functioning in a glorified body (a body that never needs rest or has a bad day) (3) serving in a community of fully dedicated Believers who speak nothing but encouragement to one another and genuinely esteem each other in love (4) completely surrounded by waves of the glory of God and (5) having daily communion with the Father, Son and Holy Spirit in person, not by faith. God has truly saved the *"Best wine for last"* (Jn.2:10). Paul's declaration about *"All things becoming new"* is probably one of the biggest understatements in scripture.

When you begin to read and see your Bible through a futuristic lens, life takes on an entirely new dimension of understanding. I hope you find that tip useful in your pursuit of fresh insight from the Word of God. I call that *"telescoping truth."* There are literally hundreds of verses that can be applied with that concept in mind.

> *Then I, John, saw the holy city, New Jerusalem, coming down out of heaven from God, **prepared as a bride adorned for her husband***
> *(Rev.21:2)*

This is an awesome word picture of how Jesus is preparing to bless His people. We are given enough details to know that this city will be God's most creative masterpiece. This city has no rivals and will capture the hearts and imagination of all who see and enter it. Some have aptly called this eternal city "the beauty realm." The beauty realm is God's highest expression of His glory. This city will be full of that glory and majesty. This is the final destination of every Believer. An ounce of revelation concerning this heavenly reality can carry the weakest heart through the deepest waters of affliction. This exalted view of the coming glorious eternal city is what prompted the Apostle Paul to write, *"For I consider that the sufferings of this present time are not worthy to be compared with the glory which shall be revealed in us"* (Rom 8:18-19).

> **He who overcomes shall inherit all things,**
> *and I will be his God and he shall be My son*
> *(Rev.21:7)*

I think the reference here to those who overcome and the promise that they will inherit all things begs the question, "Exactly what things are we talking about?" I believe this is a reference to what was promised earlier in the Book of Revelation in chapters two and three. It's like God saying, "I meant what I promised and just want you to know that I am serious." I will list these specific promises. Please do not lose sight of the fact that these promises are for everyone who overcomes. Some have made these applicable to an elite group of Believers. I take issue with that interpretation and would broaden it to say that the phrase *"He who overcomes"* applies to every saint who is allowed to participate in the first resurrection and who receives a glorified body. I see no super-class of Christians anywhere in scripture. Certainly, as mentioned earlier, there will be a distinction made in terms of eternal rewards. Each will receive according to how they managed the grace of God (gifts, abilities, resources, opportunities, etc.), that was freely lavished upon them. There are no losers in heaven. All are extremely blessed and will continue to be blessed throughout eternity.

Here are the promises given to those who love God and who are not ashamed to call Him their Father. I encourage you to take a moment and meditate on them. Imagine yourself personally receiving each one of these glorious promises. These are for every Believer who *"Endures to the end"* (Matt.24:13).

*To him who overcomes I will give to eat from
the tree of life, which is in the midst of the
Paradise of God
(Rev.2:7)*

*He who overcomes shall not be hurt by the
second death
(Rev. 2:11)*

*To him who overcomes I will give some of
the hidden manna to eat. And I will give him
a white stone, and on the stone a new name
written which no one knows except him who
receives it
(Rev.2:17)*

*And he who overcomes, and keeps My works
until the end, to him I will give power over
the nations – (27) He shall rule them with a
rod of iron; they shall be dashed to pieces
like the potter's vessels -- as I also have
received from My Father; (28) and I will
give him the morning star
(Rev.2:26-28)*

*He who overcomes shall be clothed in white
garments, and I will not blot out his name
from the Book of Life; but I will confess his
name before My Father and before His
angels
(Rev.3:5)*

*He who overcomes, I will make him a pillar
in the temple of My God, and he shall go out
no more. I will write on him the name of My
God and the name of the city of My God, the
New Jerusalem, which comes down out of
heaven from My God. And I will write on him
My new name
(Rev.3:12)*

*To him who overcomes I will grant to sit with
Me on My throne, as I also overcame and sat
down with My Father on His throne
(Rev.3:21)*

*Its gates shall not be shut at all by day [there
shall be no night there]
(Rev.21:25)*

The New Earth

Although no other information seems to follow, we do know that this city is resting on the *"new earth"* (Rev.21:1). We are also told that there are twelve gates which are located around each quadrant of the city. Biblical gates serve two purposes: (1) they allow the residents a fixed point at which to enter and exit the city and (2) they provide security (keep unwanted people out). We will not be confined to the city but will be permitted to visit the *"new earth."* The gates are specifically mentioned so that we will be aware of that fact. This may be a tip-off that some of our work assignments will be outside the city. There is no mention of what the *"new earth"* will look like but it is safe to assume it will be the most spectacular real estate man has ever seen. I'm sure it will serve as a source of endless fascination. It will be a serious upgrade from even the Garden of Eden, which we know was startling.

> *And there shall be no more curse, but the throne of God and of the Lamb shall be in it, and His servants shall serve Him.* (4) **They shall see His face,** *and His name shall be on their foreheads*
> *(Rev.22:3-4)*

Throughout the Bible there has been a prohibition against men seeing the face of God. This was not because God did not want us to see Him but was an issue of preservation. If He exposed His Holy nature to our sinful nature there would be an immediate need for a funeral because we would never survive the encounter.

Notice that this passage also gives us information about the precious seal of his ownership. He will personally write His name on our foreheads. God wants us to know that we are His throughout all eternity. This is our destiny in God and this revelation can be ours in measure now. This is why Paul encouraged the church to *"Set their affections on things above, not on things on the earth"* (Col.3:2). You can never live life the same once this realm becomes part of your daily meditation.

> *Behold, I am coming quickly! Blessed is he who keeps the words of the prophecy of this book*
> *(Rev.22:7)*

> *Blessed are those who do His commandments that they may have the right to the tree of life, and may enter through the gates into the city*
> *(Rev.22:14)*

I will leave you with these words as they are both fitting and powerful. Our future destiny will be determined by how seriously we take this admonition. The plans and purposes that God has in store for those that love Him are literally out of this world.

Final Note to the Reader

I have tried to help you see things through an entirely new lens. I hope this paradigm shift has been helpful. Please know that I have put my heart into this work and that the Lord has been speaking to me throughout this entire journey. Do not mistake that statement as a subtle attempt to authorize everything that is contained in this document. That is not my point. My wife and I have been in seclusion in a mountain cabin for most of this writing. We have done so because we wanted as few distractions as possible in order to hear as clearly as possible. We have fasted, prayed and sought to produce the purest version of the last days that our extremely limited abilities would allow.

This book was not written to be a doctrinal statement of the last days. Nor is it in my heart to attempt to prove I am right and therefore belittle the sincere work of other end time authors. That motivation has never entered my heart. Not only would that be carnal but it would be counter-productive to the end time purposes of God. My heart's desire is to help prepare a generation for the soon-coming of our Lord Jesus Christ. He is worthy of our best efforts to offer Him a life of passionate devotion. The reader is always the best judge of how successful these attempts have been. The goal of this book is more than simply imparting new information. Experience has taught me that most Believers already possess more biblical data than they know how to apply. My bride and I hope and earnestly pray that you will come away from reading this book with a deeper desire to become a lover of God and an earnest seeker of His Word. Everything else will pass away, but His Word will abide forever (1 Pet.1:23).

 Jim Maher is the founder and president of New Song International Ministries, a ministry dedicated to train, equip, and raise up worshippers in the spirit of the tabernacle of David. His teachings on intimacy with God and the last day church have inspired many to press into a deeper walk with their heavenly Bridegroom.

New Song International Ministries is a multi-faceted ministry that purposes to be a funding mechanism to assist financing and facilitating the end time prayer movement. Funds received are distributed to individual intercessors needing financial assistance as they fulfill their calling to stand in the gap in a full time capacity.

New Song International Ministries has established an *Anna Fund* with the goal of raising over $1,000,000 to be disbursed among hundreds of God's precious saints. All monies received are sown directly into the support of the night and day prayer movement in America and Israel. Donations are tax deductible.

Contact Information

New Song Ministries
4103 E. 107th Street
Kansas City, MO 64137
Ph: 816-765-2928
E-mail: newsongministries@sbcglobal.net

Please make checks payable to:
New Song Ministries
"Anna Fund" (in memo)